The Diversity of Religions

J. A. DINOIA, O.P.

The Diversity of Religions

A CHRISTIAN PERSPECTIVE

THE CATHOLIC UNIVERSITY OF AMERICA PRESS
WASHINGTON, D.C.

The paper used in this publication meets the minimum requirements of American National Standards for Information Science—Permanence of Paper for Printed Library materials, ANSI Z39.48-1984.
∞

LIBRARY OF CONGRESS
CATALOGING-IN-PUBLICATION DATA

DiNoia, J. A., 1943
The diversity of religions : a Christian perspective / by J. A. DiNoia.
p. cm.
Includes bibliographical references and index.
1. Christianity and other religions. 2. Theology—Methodology. 3. Dialogue—Religious aspects—Christianity. 4. Religious pluralism. I. Title.
BR127.D56 1992
261.2—dc20
91-33001
ISBN 0-8132-0763-0 (alk. paper)
ISBN 0-8132-0769-X (pbk.)

For my mother and
in memory of my father

Contents

Preface

This book invites theologians and other concerned Christians to take a fresh look at the issues posed for Christian communities by their commitment to engage in dialogue with Buddhist, Hindu, Muslim, and Jewish communities.

Prevailing positions in the field of theology of religions for the most part focus their energies on allowing for the possibility of salvation outside the ambit of Christianity. Allied in their rejection of exclusivism (the view that salvation requires explicit faith in Christ prior to death), inclusivists (e.g., Karl Rahner and Jacques Dupuis) and pluralists (e.g., John Hick and Paul Knitter) deploy various theological and philosophical strategies to allow for the salvation of the members of other religious communities. Inclusivists espouse some version of the view that all religious communities implicitly aim at the salvation that the Christian community most adequately commends, or at least that salvation is a present possibility for the members of other religious communities. Pluralists contend that all religious communities in effect aim at salvation, but under a variety of tradition-specific descriptions.

To be sure, the concern that fuels inclusivist and pluralist proposals is well warranted. Addressing the participants at the 1990 assembly of the Pontifical Council for Interreligious Dialogue, Pope John Paul II clearly stated this concern: "Much careful theological investigation still has to be done regarding the relation between the Church and other religions. The question of how God accomplishes the salvation of all those who call upon him through the unique mediation of Christ is one which demands the continued attention of the Church: likewise the work of the Spirit of Christ in the members of other religions."[1]

But the assumption that other religions are seeking salvation has led inclusivists and pluralists to address this concern in ways that blur distinctive features of the religious landscape. Major religious communities commend a variety of ultimate aims of life that coincide neither with one another nor with what Christians mean by salvation. It would be desirable for Christian theology of religions to affirm Christian confidence in the universality of salvation in a way that gave full value to the diversity of aims of life and consequent patterns of life commended by other religious communities.

This objective takes on special urgency in view of the embrace of interreligious dialogue on the part of most Christian communities. The determination to engage in such dialogue entails a readiness to take the distinctive doctrines of other religious communities seriously. Can Christian theology of religions affirm the universality of salvation in a way that is consistent with Christian determination to engage in interreligious dialogue?

That question guides the inquiry undertaken in this book. Chapter 1 maps something of the philosophical, doctrinal, and historical contours of the inquiry. The interaction of one religious community with other religious communities is governed in part by the traditional doctrines about other religious communities which are part of its heritage. Part of the task of Christian theologians today is to develop their communities' doctrines about other religions in ways that will affirm the availability of salvation and support participation in interreligious dialogue.

Subsequent chapters sketch the outlines of a proposed Christian theology of religions fit for these purposes. It is distinguished from other recent proposals in this area by its endeavor to take alien religious doctrines into account in developing formulations

1. *Bulletin* of the Pontifical Council for Interreligious Dialogue, 74, XXV (1990), 120–21.

of traditional Christian doctrines about other religions, especially those concerning the universality of salvation. As chapter 2 argues, since many current positions define the entire agenda of Christian theology of religions in terms of the issue of the "salvation" of non-Christians, they underestimate the significance of the varieties of religious aims commended by other traditions or minimize the distinctiveness of Christian claims in these areas. The theology of religions outlined in chapter 3 strives, without prejudice to central Christian doctrines, to do justice to the distinctive religious claims and patterns of life commended by other traditions. Such a theology of religions serves better than many recent proposals to support Christian participation in interreligious dialogue. Chapter 4 takes Christian theology of religions into interreligious dialogue in order to explore the patterns of argument appropriate in that setting and consistent with Christian doctrines about other religions. As chapter 5 makes explicit, the argument of this book is experimental and exploratory. It tests the viability of a Christian theology of religions keen on doing justice to the doctrines of other communities and to the arguments likely to be advanced in their support.

Christian interaction with Hindu, Buddhist, Jewish, and Muslim communities, rather than with, say, African or Native American traditions, is at the center of attention in this book. In contrast with local or native religions, the major traditions pose highly ramified alternatives to Christian belief and practice, and advance similarly universalistic claims. Concentration on major religions thus serves to focus the issues posed by religious interaction more sharply. Among the major religions, Buddhist traditions supply most of the illustrations introduced to support the argument of this book. This choice reflects the interests and competence of the author.

Footnotes have been kept to an absolute minimum so that the reader can follow the argument of the book without unnecessary distractions. Only direct quotations and citations of the work of others are identified in the footnotes. References to supporting literature and alternative positions occur in the Bibliographical Notes at the end of the book, arranged by chapter and following the sequence of the argument.

I am grateful to many people who helped me to bring this book to completion, especially those who read all or parts of this manuscript at various stages in its long journey to publication, in particular the members of the Yale-Washington Theology Group (Jim Buckley, Mike Root, Louis Pressman, Ron Thiemann, Bill Placher, Bill Werpehowski, George Hunsinger, Tom Tracy, and Bruce Marshall). Special thanks are due to George Lindbeck, William Christian, Sr., Louis Dupré, Gavin D'Costa, Chester Gillis, Joseph Egan, John P. Reeder, Jr., John Janaro, Nicholas Halligan, O.P., Sister Mary Catherine Wolfe, O.P., and Susan Needham, editor at The Catholic University of America Press, who offered invaluable suggestions and assistance. I thank the editors and publishers of *Religious Studies, Theological Studies, The Thomist,* the University of Notre Dame Press, and Orbis Books for kindly granting permission to reprint reworked sections of previously published essays here.[2] I am particularly indebted to the Dominican nuns and their many friends in Elmira, New York, who provided a haven during the year in which the first draft of this book was completed.

Feast of the Assumption, 1991
Washington, D.C.

2. "The Doctrines of a Religious Community about Other Religions," *Religious Studies* 19 (1982–83), 293–307; "Philosophical Theology in the Perspective of Religious Diversity," *Theological Studies* 49 (1988), 401–16; "Implicit Faith, General Revelation and the State of Non-Christians," *Thomist* 47 (1983), 209–41; "Varieties of Religious Aims: Beyond Exclusivism, Inclusivism and Pluralism," in *Theology and Dialogue,* ed. Bruce Marshall (Notre Dame: University of Notre Dame Press, 1991), 247–72; "Pluralist Theology of Religions: Pluralistic or Non-Pluralistic?" in *Christian Uniqueness Reconsidered,* ed. Gavin D'Costa (Maryknoll: Orbis Books, 1990), 119–34.

The Diversity of Religions

CHAPTER ONE

Christian Doctrines about Other Religions

THE WANDERER Subhada once asked Gautama the Buddha whether teachers other than the Buddha himself could be relied upon to guide their disciples to Nirvana. The Buddha responded that indeed they could be, but only if their teachings included the essential elements of the Excellent Eightfold Path.[1]

Subhada's question typifies the concern sometimes felt by members of one religious community when they contemplate the situation of nonmembers. Buddhists teach that Nirvana can be attained only by following the Excellent Eightfold Path. Such a claim is not odd. Religious communities that propose specific goals for human life as a whole—as Buddhists, Christians, and others clearly seem to do—have generally not shown themselves to be indifferent about the means to reach these goals. The capacities to attain and enjoy certain ends of life depend in large measure on courses of life shaped by the particular practices, goods, and beliefs commended by religious communities in their main teachings. Given the importance of the aim of life that a commu-

1. See the *Mahāparinibbānasutta* (5, 23–30) in *Dialogues of the Buddha*, part 2, trans. T. W. Rhys Davids and C. A. F. Rhys Davids, (London: Pali Text Society, 1910), 164–69.

nity pursues and commends, its members are anxious to know the chances outsiders have of attaining it as well. Can someone who doesn't follow the path reach the goal?

The Buddha's answer is typical of the kind of response that religious communities offer in such circumstances. Even when other teachings about the true aim of life and the path to it are regarded as erroneous, it is often thought by one community that other communities could possess some doctrines that, if discerned and followed, would advance their members along the right path nonetheless. Thus, it need not be a sign of arrogance that a religious community teaches that a certain course of life is necessary for the attainment of the true aim of life. Nor is it intolerant to teach that other courses can delay, divert, or impede human beings who might otherwise be set on the right course. Attainment of the true aim of life is, after all, a matter of considerable importance.

Occasions often arise when a member of one religious community, like Subhada, asks the teachers in his community about the members of other religious communities: What do we have to say about other religions? What is the value of their beliefs and ways of life as compared with ours? How are we to regard other religious people? How are we to act toward them?

Such questions might come up in circumstances of actual contact between members of one community and the members of other communities. Imagine a Muslim returned from travels in the Indian subcontinent, or a Catholic contemplating marriage with a Buddhist. Subhada's question arose from his encounters with other teachers besides the Buddha. On the other hand, questions about other religions might reflect a more hypothetical interest, kindled perhaps by the study of the religious literatures of distant cultures or by some scholarly inquiry about religion. Imagine a Jewish student reading the *Upanishads,* or a Buddhist scholar studying medieval exegesis of the Bible.

If a religious community has answers to questions of this kind or is prepared to venture some, then it proposes what might be [achieving] purity of insight." Commenting on this passage, the Buddhist scholar Phra Khantipalo remarks that "though there are many teachings in the world, they lead either in directions opposed to Nirvana (materialism, Communism), or, at most, only to the lower heavens gained by good works (and open therefore to the laymen of all religions) or to the higher states of bliss (attainable by the saints of, for instance, Christianity, Hinduism, and Islam)."

This assessment of other teachings reflects not "exclusiveness" or intolerance, Khantipalo insists, but simply a straightforward declaration that proper tools and developed skills are needed to accomplish a defined task. "Only in Buddhadharma is that wisdom taught which frees one completely from the round of births." The Buddhist attitudes of tolerance that Khantipalo advocates echo the teaching of the Buddha, who was critical without being intolerant of other teachers who, "not having the correct method . . . to effect liberation, . . . aimed amiss and so came to have many and diverse goals."[2]

Such remarks are representative of many that could be cited from the canonical and commentatorial literature of Buddhist communities. They render explicit what seems to be a basic assumption of this literature. The Dharma that is taught in Buddhist communities—that is, the truth about the path to Nirvana—constitutes a teaching of universal scope and applicability. Buddhist communities commend to their members and to outsiders the pursuit of the true aim of life, an account of the conditions of human existence relevant to achieving it, and the pattern of life that assures its attainment and enjoyment. For this reason, whatever is taught in other religious communities can be appraised on the basis of the Dharma.

The Buddha's teaching exemplifies a persistent feature of the traditions of most religious communities. Although there are dis-

2. Phra Khantipalo, *Tolerance: A Study from Buddhist Sources* (London: Rider & Company, 1964), 114–15.

agreements among the world's major religious communities about what constitutes the true aim of life, they seem to be one in commending to their members and to outsiders distinctive overall aims of life and patterns of life fit to their pursuit, attainment, and enjoyment.

In Buddhist communities, for example, the possibility of attaining Nirvana, or liberation from the round of rebirths, begins with aiming at it. That is to say, in order at least to have the chance of enjoying the true aim of life at some time in the future, one's present life must be pointed in the right direction. Buddhist communities, in the first place, teach their members that Nirvana is that upon which they should set their sights. Alternative conceptions of the true aim of life can be shown to be partial or incorrect, as Khantipalo suggests above. According to Buddhist teachers, "wrong views" about such matters must yield to "right views" if one is to make real progress along the path to liberation and enlightenment. In addition, Buddhist teachings furnish an enormously detailed account (further "right views") of the conditions of human existence that enmesh people in the round of rebirths. Most important of all, Buddhist practical doctrines present the method—handily described as the Excellent Eightfold Path—by which these conditions can be transcended and Nirvana the more surely attained.

Analogies from nonreligious pursuits throw some light on the structure of doctrines about the aim of life, and the pattern that life should take in view of such aims. Consider the example of a cellist who seeks to play Bach's Unaccompanied Cello Suites well. This objective shapes the development of a range of physical, intellectual, and affective dispositions in the cellist. The objective is intrinsic to the activity of cello playing and serves to define it in a way that, say, the more extrinsic purposes of winning the applause of an audience or earning a livelihood through recording are not. The strenuous schedule of practice, which the cellist undertakes in order at least to maintain, if not to exceed, a certain level of performance, transforms her capacities in a more or less stable manner. Having taken as her aim the successful performance of works like the Cello Suites, she becomes a certain kind of person, one who possesses a range of skills and dispositions that afford additional experiences of creative accomplishments and satisfactions.

The connections between religious aims of life and the patterns they call forth are similar. "Nirvana" designates not an extrinsic reward bestowed on someone who successfully follows the Excellent Eightfold Path but an achievement whose enjoyment the Excellent Eightfold Path makes possible. By undertaking to seek Nirvana and to have one's capacities and dispositions shaped by the pattern of life commended by the community, one becomes the sort of person who can attain and, more importantly, enjoy that which Nirvana entails. This intrinsic connection between aims of life and patterns of life is evident in the teachings of other religious communities as well. Fellowship with the Blessed Trinity, Torah holiness, the garden of delights—these are some of the terms by which the Christian, Judaic, and Muslim communities respectively define the true aim of life. In these communities, it is understood that the possibility of attaining and enjoying the goal of life in the future depends upon the shape that life in the present takes. For this reason, religious communities place great emphasis in their practical doctrines on the acquisition (by grace or personal effort, as the case may be) and development of appropriate dispositions for enjoying the true aim of life.

The overall point of religious teachings thus seems to be the cultivation of a pattern of life in view of some definition of the true aim of life as a whole. Such an aim is defined in connection with an ascription of unrestricted value to a particular state of being (liberation or enlightenment, in the case of Buddhism) or to some existent (Allah in Islam, or the Blessed Trinity in Christianity). The members of a religious community are taught to orient the whole of their lives to the attainment of union with some object or existent or of enjoyment of some state of being. This aim is worth seeking above all others that could be imagined or pursued—and is thus, by implication, worthy of pursuit by all human beings without exception.

In view of its definition of the true aim of life, a religious community maintains well-developed conceptions about the shape human lives ought to take in order to attain and enjoy this aim. The capacities to attain and enjoy certain kinds of ends of life depend in large measure on courses of life shaped by the particular practices, values, and beliefs commended by religious communities in their central doctrines. As Phra Khantipalo notes, it is not exclusivistic pretensions that compel a religious community to teach that a certain course of life is necessary for focusing upon and attaining the true aim of life, or that other courses of life can delay or impede human beings from pursuing the right course. The Christian claim that there is no salvation except through Jesus Christ, or the Buddhist claim that there is no attainment of Nirvana except in the following of the Excellent Eightfold Path, reflects not an unwarranted exclusivism on the part of these communities but the seriousness with which each regards the true aim of life and the means necessary to attain and enjoy it.

To enjoy Nirvana, one has to become a certain kind of person. Does it follow that, if one has sought union with the Blessed Trinity or Torah holiness, then the attainment and enjoyment of Nirvana is precluded? This is as complex a question for Buddhist communities as are its analogues for other communities.

A community's doctrines about the true aim of life normally impart both urgency and caution to its account of the access to this aim afforded to nonmembers by alien religious teachings. But if a particular community were to assume that other communities foster aims identical to its own, or that the other aims of life are as worthy of pursuit as its own, or that the patterns of life commended by other communities advance their members to the true aim of life—then questions about the state and prospects of nonmembers and the value of their beliefs would presumably lose urgency. But Christian doctrines (as well as those of other major traditions) seem to preclude such assumptions. For this reason, the question arises: what chance do other religious persons have of attaining life's true aim despite their persistence in patterns of life that seem to point them in different and possibly wrong directions?

As William A. Christian has observed, "There seems to be a deep-seated tendency in the major religious communities to develop a comprehensive pattern of life . . . which bears on all human interests . . . and on all situations in which human beings find themselves."[3] Deploying the analogy of a cultural-linguistic scheme, George A. Lindbeck has made a similar point by drawing attention to the ways in which religious traditions mold the whole of the life and experience of their adherents.[4] Each of the world's great religions seems to direct its adherents to some ultimate aim of life, and each proposes some pattern which life as a whole ought to take in view of that aim. Thus the entire outlook of the pious Christian has come to be shaped by the fundamental conviction that a good life is one lived in seeking to be in union with God and with other human beings in him. In effect, the whole burden of the message of the Scriptures as these have come to be interpreted in the traditions of his community is to foster this aim across all the interests and occasions of life. The prayers and stories, customs and rites, beliefs and ethical teachings of the Christian community have the Triune God as their focus and aim.

The traditions of religious communities are practical and comprehensive in this sense. They foster distinctive patterns of life to which their members strive, with varying degrees of proficiency, to conform, in view of some definition of the true aim of life.

In the course of fostering their distinctive patterns of life, religious communities generally teach something specific. Whether rules for meditation or credal formulas, "religious doctrines" are

3. William A. Christian, Sr., *Doctrines of Religious Communities* (New Haven: Yale University Press, 1987), 186.

4. George A. Lindbeck, *The Nature of Doctrine* (Philadelphia: Westminster, 1984), 32–41.

those elements of discourse in religious communities in which some truth is proposed for belief, or some good as worth seeking, or some course of action for adoption. In addition to other forms of speech—confessions, stories, prayers, invocations, blessings, and so on—doctrines occur as a regular feature of the characteristic discourse of most religious communities. The whole set of teachings in which the distinctive pattern of life of a religious community is conveyed can be called simply its body or scheme of doctrines.

The body of doctrines of a religious community can be said to teach a pattern of life of which certain valuations (e.g., "God alone is holy"), certain recommendations of inward and outward courses of action (e.g., "Strive to live in union with the Holy Trinity" or "Show love in dealing with neighbors"), and certain beliefs (e.g., "God created the world from nothing" or "Jesus Christ saves us from our sins") are constituent.

Thus, for example, the Christian scheme contains doctrines that convey its basic religious valuation and its chief recommendations for the shape life ought to have in view of this valuation. One way of expressing the comprehensive aim Christianity proposes for human life would be to say that the whole of life should be directed to the attainment of salvation, which consists in a relationship of union with the Blessed Trinity. Ingredient in this central practical doctrine is an ascription of inherent value to God: God is good without reference to any further object or existent, for it is only in his presence that an intrinsically valuable state of being can be attained. Christian doctrines express this basic religious valuation in a variety of ways—all in order to give point to the recommendation of a comprehensive aim for life and to many other practical doctrines as well. Other central Christian doctrines express beliefs about the human condition, about the necessity of a divine initiative if human beings are to be able to advance toward the true aim of life, about the exercise of this initiative in the history of Israel and in the career of Jesus Christ, and about its continuation in the Christian community.

In some historical situations a religious community may show little or no interest in other religious communities and their members. But contact and interaction with other religious people is likely to stimulate some concern about the worth of their beliefs and practices. In the history of religions such interaction has occurred in the great variety of circumstances prevailing in warfare, trade, missionary ventures, and the like. Such interaction has prompted most of the major world religions to develop some teachings about other religions, either individually or *en bloc.*

Where a religious community has had occasion to teach something about other religious communities and their members, it develops "doctrines about other religions." These doctrines appraise the patterns of life fostered by other religions and commend policies and attitudes to be adopted to other religions and their adherents. In these doctrines a religious community's central doctrines are interpreted and developed in ways that will generate valuations, beliefs, and policies with regard to other religions. Such doctrines follow from its own central doctrines and address circumstances of interaction (if there be any) between its members and the members of other religious communities. The presumption here is that a community's doctrines permit such developments. That is to say, among the community's doctrines there are some principles that allow the community to take notice (logically speaking) of alien religious claims and to give some account of them in relation to its own primary doctrines.

A rough but useful distinction can be drawn between doctrines about other religions *qua* religions (as systems of beliefs or patterns of life) and doctrines about the adherents of other religions (as fellow human beings or nonmembers).

A community's doctrines about other religions *qua* religions assert something to be true or to be valued about them, or recommend some course of action to be undertaken in their regard. Thus a religious community's scheme of doctrines might teach some doctrines of the following form:

Other religions teach some true and right doctrines.
Other religions can advance their members toward the attainment of the true aim of life.
The traditions of other religions should be studied and esteemed.

Note that doctrines about other religions *qua* religions in a particular religious community (R1) could refer to all other religious communities as a group, as in the examples above, or to individual religious communities singly as in the following examples:

R2 is fulfilled (or superseded, or abrogated) by R1.
R3 is a thoroughly corrupt religion.

There would be various possibilities here, depending on the range of contact one community has with other communities.

In addition to a religious community's doctrines about other religions *qua* religions, there can be doctrines about the *members* of other religious communities. These doctrines assert something to be the case or to be good or deficient in the religious and moral states of the members of other religious communities, or propose some course of inward or outward action to be adopted in dealings with them. A community's doctrines about the members of other religious communities could refer to all such persons as a group or to the members of some particular religious community. Thus a community might teach some doctrines of the following forms:

Members of other religious communities can perform good actions conducive to the attainment of the true aim of life.
The members of R2 should be persuaded of the errors of the doctrines they hold.
Engage in dialogue with the members of other religious communities.

As will become apparent, the distinction between doctrines about other religions *qua* religions and doctrines about the members of other religious communities is useful for clarifying the different ways a community's central doctrines come to bear on the development of its doctrines about other religions.

Like other teachings in a religious community—including some important ones—its doctrines about other religions need not have received official formulation in its creeds and codes but may nevertheless have acquired certain standard uses, which apply beyond the concrete circumstances that occasioned their emergence. Among such uses several are worth noting. First, doctrines about other religions that were originally elaborated in order to guide a religious community in its dealings with one religious community can supply precedents for its relations with others as they are newly encountered. Indeed, its doctrines about other religions can eventually serve to shape its assessments of all groups, teachings, and individuals that do not fall within the bounds of its membership and of adherence to its teachings. In this way a religious community's doctrines about other religions come to be applied to thought systems that are only in a borderline sense religious and to individuals who adhere to such systems, or who do not profess allegiance to any explicitly religious community or body of beliefs and practices. Next, although a religious community's doctrines about other religions are for the most part addressed to its own members or to questions they may raise, such doctrines may have uses in apologetic arguments constructed in order to persuade nonmembers to approve, favorably entertain, or adopt the pattern of life fostered by the community and conveyed in its doctrines. Lastly, a religious community's doctrines about other religions can have important internal uses. Such doctrines can function to explicate the point of its central doctrines in times when it has very limited contacts with the members of other religious communities. Such doctrines can come to be propounded and developed without reference to any existing communities and mainly to disclose the point of some of its central doctrines.

Nevertheless, it remains true that an important function of

such doctrines in a religious community seems to be to assess other communities' potential for advancing their members toward the true aim of life without the advantage of a fully reliable description of this aim and of the pattern of life required for its attainment. The importance of this function is certainly verified in the Christian scheme.

DOCTRINES IN THE CHRISTIAN COMMUNITY ABOUT OTHER RELIGIONS

Let us experiment with some working formulations of important Christian doctrines about other religions, both about other religions *qua* religions and about the members of other religious communities. In order to study the logic rather than the fascinating history of such doctrines, they can usefully be abstracted from the enormous classical literature on these topics, and thus from their historical contexts. The gain in conceptual clarity will perhaps make up for the loss of historical concreteness at this point. There will be occasion later in this chapter to note the varied historical settings of doctrines of this kind in the Christian community.

We can make some headway in grasping the issues posed for Christian communities by their commitment to engage in interreligious dialogue if we have in hand a framework for identifying some of the doctrines that generally guide them in their relations with other religious communities. Our goal is to discover what developments such doctrines might require when Christian theology of religions begins to take better account of the distinctive claims that other religious communities make for themselves. The outcome of this inquiry has special bearing on the questions that so preoccupy Christian theology of religions today: Can non-Christians attain salvation? Do other religious communities aim at salvation?

Consider first some Christian doctrines about other religions *qua* religions. A good place to start is with the following working formulation:

C1. Other religions teach partial truth in comparison with the fullness of truth taught in the Christian community.

Christian central doctrines can be interpreted as permitting the assertion of this doctrine in the following way.

The doctrines of revelation and inspiration are invoked in order to affirm that God can bring it about that some elements of the Christian pattern of life—perhaps even essential ones—might occur outside the bounds of the visible Christian community. Whether or not this is actually the case would call for observation and generalization. But Christians could teach that true and right doctrines may occur in other religions without adducing examples of such doctrines and without proposing any theory to explain their presence in existing (or extinct) religious traditions. Even in the absence of direct acquaintance with other religious communities, Christians could assert, as an implication of central Christian doctrines about the freedom, omnipotence, mercy, and universal providence of God, that other religions teach some true and right doctrines. In view of these doctrines it would seem inconsistent to many Christians to fix limits on the scope of God's action such that only the Christian pattern of life would be regarded as embodying true beliefs or fostering aspects of a good life.

Thus the doctrine that other religions could possess true or right teachings can be seen to articulate an implication of central Christian doctrines about the unrestricted power of God to enable human beings to discover the truth about himself and to live in accordance with that truth. But this implication would presumably need to be qualified by other central Christian doctrines about the more focused activity of God in the election of the people of Israel, in the ministry and destiny of Jesus Christ, and in the presence of the Holy Spirit in the Christian community. According to these doctrines God has made himself known in a special manner in particular times and places and has provided the means by which human beings can achieve, with greater assurance than would otherwise be possible, the true aim of life, that is, union with and participation in the life of the Trinity. A primary function of the doctrine of revelation in the Christian scheme seems to be to articulate the nature and consequences of this special communication on God's part.

The nature of this qualification and its dependence on central Christian doctrines (in addition to the doctrine of revelation) can be observed more directly by considering the following expression of another prominent Christian doctrine about other religions *qua* religions:

C2. Other religions are superseded by Christianity.

If, as the Christian scheme can plausibly be construed to teach, the true aim of life is union with the Trinity and if membership in the Christian community is the means given to attain this aim, then it would not be consistent with central Christian doctrines to ascribe to other religious communities a value equivalent to that ascribed to the Christian community. Thus, although central Christian doctrines affirm the universality of the divine salvific will, they also assert that the Christian community in its authentic forms has a privileged access to knowledge about this aim of life and to the means to attain and enjoy it. Any ascription of value to the doctrines, institutions, and forms of life of other religious communities would have to be qualified by ascriptions of inherent, intrinsic, and contributory value to the Christian community and to membership in it. This doctrine can be expressed in statements employing a variety of related but logically independent concepts among which the following figure prominently: invalidation, supersession, fulfillment, and perfection. Each of these concepts could be employed, it seems clear, in elaborating Christian doctrines about other religions in ways that would be consistent with central Christian doctrines that ascribe a unique set of valuations to the Christian community.

Another Christian doctrine about other religions develops implications of Christian convictions about the providence and universal salvific will of God:

C3. Other religions could play some role in the divine plan of salvation.

According to this doctrine, other religions could be said to exercise a preparatory role with regard to Christianity in world history, or in the history of particular cultures, or in the lifetimes of individual human beings. Insofar as the partial truth in other religions can be dispositive for the emergence or acceptance of the fullness of truth in Christianity, other religions could be said to be encompassed in the order of grace and salvation.

The Christian scheme can be interpreted as yielding three main doctrines about other religions *qua* religions. These doctrines acknowledge the partial truth (C1) and providential role (C3) of other religions without prejudice to the attribution of special properties to the Christian community in comparison with other religions (C2). Consider now some prominent Christian doctrines about the members of other religious communities.

In view of the unique valuation of the Christian community, Christian doctrines about the members of other religious communities will presumably need to account for their hoped-for salvation in part by asserting the possibility of a fellowship with the Blessed Trinity, which renders them virtually or hiddenly members of the Christian community, or God's people on earth. Consider the following statement of such a doctrine:

C4. Members of other religious communities could be in fellowship with God and thus in some hidden way be members of the Christian community.

According to central Christian doctrines about the universal salvific will of God, all human beings who have ever lived—including those who lived before the emergence of the Christian community—are called to participate in a relationship of union with

God. Some construals of Christian doctrines about these matters take it that the very existence of the universe and of humankind within it is attributable in the first place to the divine intention to enter into union with human beings. If the universal human condition is such that persons could not attain their true and divinely willed destiny without benefit of divine help, then this aid—given in Christ in a decisive way—must be accessible to all persons who have ever lived. Hence there are Christian doctrines that human beings who attain their true destiny do so only in virtue of the grace of Christ and thus only through some sort of affiliation with the community in which this grace is uniquely (though not exclusively, according to most Christian theologians) found.

Many important Christian doctrines about the members of other religious communities try to account for the possibility of a hidden fellowship with the Blessed Trinity and a virtual association with the Christian community on the part of nonmembers. Consider the following examples of Catholic formulations of such doctrines:

C5. Members of other religious communities could possess an implicit faith, which could become explicit in Christianity.

C6. Members of other religious communities could perform good actions having salvific value for them.

C5 draws upon a standard distinction made in Christian doctrines about the sacraments and means of grace between ordinary and *in voto* (that is, effectively desired) reception of sacramental grace and on the classical concept of implicit faith. C6 articulates the persistent Christian recognition of the many instances of morally upright conduct on the part of persons who are not Christians and in addition ascribes contributory (or "salvific") value to such conduct. Christian doctrines such as these express a valuation of a certain range of religious and moral states by ascribing to the members of other religious communities a hidden fellowship with God and a virtual membership in his people.

In addition to Christian doctrines about other religions that convey assertions and valuations, there are some that recommend courses of action. These practical doctrines about other religions serve to guide Christians in their dealings with other religious groups and their members. Such practical doctrines about other religions urge or enjoin the adoption of certain attitudes and policies in their regard. Examples of such practical doctrines about other religions are:

C7. Christians should engage in dialogue with the members of other religious communities.
C8. Christians should proclaim the gospel to the members of other religious communities.
C9. Christians should collaborate with the members of other religious communities in projects of common human concern.

Practical doctrines such as these would presumably receive their force from central Christian doctrines and from the valuations and assertions conveyed by doctrines about other religions *qua* religions and by doctrines about their members.

THEOLOGY OF RELIGIONS IN HISTORICAL PERSPECTIVE

Given the fairly loose structure of most schemes of doctrines, there is likely to be a considerable degree of flexibility in the way a religious community's doctrines about other religions are proposed and developed in particular orderings of its central doctrines by its expert teachers (theologians and their counterparts in nontheistic communities). Consider briefly some general features of the logic of distinctive formulations of a religious community's doctrines about other religions proposed in connection with different orderings of its central doctrines by these experts. These somewhat abstract considerations throw light on the nature and history of the activity that goes by the tag "theology of religions" in the Christian community.

Such formulations may give expression to already existing doctrines about other religions in a religious community, or be interpretations of some of its central doctrines that subsequently come to be accepted as well-formed doctrines about other religions. These formulations can be distinguished from the more or less standard traditional teachings that are embedded in its scheme of doctrines, and from authoritative formulations of such teachings (if there be any) that emanate from its official or quasi-official sources. An overall systematic account of the doctrines about other religions in a religious community (such as a "theology of religions" in Christianity) would presumably incorporate most if not all of the main formulations of such doctrines that have been elaborated in the history of the community, as well as suggest some new ones. A well-developed overall account of a religious community's doctrines about other religions would normally explicate the connections between these doctrines and its own central doctrines as well as appeal to other fields of knowledge, especially in order to propose some principles of judgment by which the doctrines and forms of life in specific other religious communities could be appraised.

Considerable variety is possible in such overall accounts as might be developed in a religious community. For example, a particular doctrine about other religions may figure more prominently in one ordering of doctrines than in another. Again, some orderings of the doctrines of a religious community may seem to work with the unexpressed rule that all explications of the doctrines of a religious community must be undertaken with a view to its doctrines about other religions and their adherents, while other orderings may disregard such doctrines entirely. Again, the connections between such doctrines and central doctrines may be explicated differently in alternative orderings of a religious community's body of doctrines. Variations like these could be fruitfully studied in the course of comparative analysis of particular orderings of the doctrines of a religious community by philosophers of religion or others interested in the logic of religious discourse.

Because a religious community's doctrines about other religions may exercise important functions in disclosing something of the overall logic of its doctrinal scheme, distinctive formulations of such doctrines by its expert teachers may be proposed with a view to projected rather than actual interaction between its members and the members of other religious communities. Rather than relationships between one religious community and other specific communities, what may be in view here is the relation between one religious community and an ideal form of religious community. The paradigmatic religion could be described in a variety of ways. The result would be a summary of the main features thought to be basic to all actually existing religious communities, or a stipulative definition of the structures of an ideal religious community (aspects of which are partially instanced in particular existing communities), or a dimension of the innate or acquired dispositions of human persons, or a structure or set of structures in the organization, legitimation, and maintenance of social and cultural systems. To put this point more succinctly, in this case a religious community's doctrines about other religions come to be formulated with a view to some general theory of religion. Such formulations may be developed mainly for internal purposes, in order to clarify the point or draw out certain implications or propose an interpretation of some central doctrines in a religious community. Formulations of this kind may or may not prove serviceable in the circumstances of interaction between one religious community and others; their usefulness here would depend upon such matters as how adequately they encompass the doctrines of existing religious communities.

The Christian doctrines about other religions summarized earlier (C1–6) originated in particular historical situations in the Christian community as doctrines expressing valuations and assertions about particular religions and their adherents. Thus, the literature in which they were first propounded manifests extensive and detailed knowledge of the classical and ethnic polytheisms, the royal cults, the mystery religions, and the sophisticated religio-philosophical systems (represented by developments of Platonism and Stoicism, for example) prevalent in Hellenistic societies of late antiquity. Taking its lead from the Scriptures, this early literature framed its acknowledgment of the partial truth and its rejection of errors of other traditions and patterns of life in terms of specific judgments about the beliefs and practices of particular cults and philosophical schools. Authors like Justin Martyr (in his *Apologies*), Clement of Alexandria (in his *Protrepticus, Pedagogus,* and *Stromateis*), or Augustine (especially in the *City of God*) wrote—with respect or disapproval as the case may be—about doctrines with which they had been acquainted firsthand or to which they themselves at one time had subscribed.

The Christian community's teachings about Judaism's providential relationship to it were generalized and modified in this literature to explicate the invalidation, supersession, and fulfillment of all the religions of classical antiquity (in doctrines like C2) specifically with regard to their particular theistic, ethical, and soteriological doctrines. Ascriptions of a providential role to other religions, and expressions of confidence about their adherents' eternal salvation (in C3–6) reflected the conviction on the part of early Christian writers that most of the persons and the religions in their experience seemed to seek the salvation that Christ alone in fact could assure them.

The doctrines about other religions that were to become standard in the Christian community were thus originally propounded in circumstances of religious interaction in which explicit attention to the doctrines and forms of life of particular traditions was unavoidable. In the literature of this period, Christian doctrines about other religions almost always had specific referents in view. The literature of Christian antiquity abounds in formulations in which doctrines first propounded with reference to Judaism came to be applied to the other religions and religious philosophies with which Christians were engaged in dialogue and debate. But in much of its subsequent literature the Christian community's doctrines about other religions were for the most part propounded independently of valuations and assertions having for their specific referents any religious traditions or their adherents. This development is understandable. Throughout most of its later history the Christian community rarely experienced circumstances of religious interaction comparable to those of late antiquity. Not until well into modern times would such circumstances again obtain on a broad scale.

During much of its history the Christian community's interaction with other religious communities was limited in scope. Hence its theologians had little occasion to take the doctrines and patterns of life of other religions specifically into account in developing Christian doctrines about other religions. With the gradual eclipse of classical polytheism, with the establishment of Christianity as the religion of the Byzantine empire, and with the Christian appropriation of many of the religious and philosophical ideas of the Hellenistic world, only the Judaic community retained a significant religious identity in the midst of an enveloping Christendom. During large portions of Christian history, Islam appears to have been regarded as something of a Christian heresy rather than as a distinctive religious community. The religions of the nomadic tribes at the edges of civilization were thought to represent versions of the thoroughly corrupt polytheism increasingly on the same wane throughout the empire itself and were dealt with accordingly. Well into the middle ages and beyond, therefore, Christian doctrines about other religions were regularly invoked to clarify the point of its own central doctrines or to authorize vigorous and far-reaching missionary endeavors. The prominence of formulations asserting the supersession and fulfillment of other religions (C2) along with generally negative assessments of other religions and convictions about the difficulty of attaining salvation without explicit faith lent considerable urgency to the Christian missionary enterprise. Where they occur at all, acknowledgments of the worth of other religions (in doctrines like C1 and C3) had about them a speculative and hypothetical character. These doctrines, as well as those about presumed members of other religious communities (like C4–6), were affirmed in much of Christian literature after late antiquity as implications of central doctrines. Such doctrines would retain their plausibility as descriptions of non-Christians in circumstances where there was little direct contact with the members of other religious communities.

The ages of exploration and colonialism marked the beginning of a decisive shift in the circumstances of religious interaction to which the Christian community had become accustomed over the course of more than a thousand years. The discovery of new lands brought with it a growing realization of the great variety of distinctive religious beliefs and practices and of previously unimagined numbers of human beings beyond the reach of Christian proclamation. In part this realization served as a stimulus to the Christian missionary enterprise. Another important long-range effect was to bring Christian doctrines about other religions into new prominence. Specifically, Christian theologians were now being called upon to develop the traditional doctrines about other religions in such a way as to make them suitable in circumstances vastly more complex than any experienced by Christian communities in previous periods—late antiquity included.

Thus modern-day Christian communities inherit formulations of doctrines about other religions originally proposed to account for particular religious traditions but subsequently developed mainly for internal purposes or in endorsement of evangelization policies. Christian communities generally seem to suppose that these doctrines can continue to be propounded for standard internal purposes and in the other ways they have customarily been used. But when relations with other religious communities are defined at least in part by the policy of dialogue, Christian communities for which these traditional doctrines about other religions continue to be authoritative will need to develop them in ways that could take account of the distinctive doctrinal claims put forward by other religious communities. This task poses a formidable challenge to Christian theology of religions.

As we shall observe, the setting of interreligious dialogue provides a context well suited to exploring the nature of this challenge as well as the prospects for developing Christian doctrines about other religions along the lines required by present circumstances. For, dialogue is a form of conversation in which the distinctive doctrinal claims religions make and support emerge with particular clarity.

CHRISTIAN THEOLOGY OF RELIGIONS AND INTERRELIGIOUS DIALOGUE

In circumstances of interaction between the members of one religious community and the members of other religious communities, assessments of particular features of the discourse and practice of these other communities are likely to be required. Detailed appraisals of this kind would presumably need to move beyond considerations suggested by a religious community's central doctrines and its general doctrines about other religions in order to develop some specific doctrines about other religions. The situation of interreligious dialogue, for example, certainly appears to involve circumstances of interaction of this kind.

Thus, for a religious community to make progress in developing such doctrines, internal doctrinal considerations of its own would not be sufficient. It would presumably need to be informed about the doctrines of other communities and about the arguments advanced for these doctrines in these communities. Its governing doctrines would have to permit developments of this kind by allowing it to take notice (logically speaking) of claims to truth and rightness that arise outside its ambit and independently of its doctrines. In this way its members would be equipped to assess the valuations, precepts, and beliefs asserted or recommended in the bodies of doctrines of other individual communities. In the course of such assessments, it might turn out that some of the doctrines of these communities are judged to be identical with some of its own (and thus not strictly alien); others might be opposed to some of its own. Others still might turn out to be consistent with its body of doctrines but not identical with any one of its own doctrines. There are many possibilities here. The formation of specific doctrines about other religions such as these involves attention (logically) to the particular doctrines of other religious communities as these are proposed and argued for by their members.

Doctrinal considerations thus influence and define one community's relations with others. Conversely, interaction with other religious communities can have an impact on the internal development of a community's own central doctrines—if its governing doctrines allow. Taking notice of the doctrines of other religious communities and developing doctrines about their doctrines may suggest some reappraisals of a community's primary doctrines and stimulate new understandings of their meaning and scope. Furthermore, changing circumstances may require reformulation of a community's inherited doctrines about other religions. In part this is because the connections between such doctrines and its own central doctrines are not hard and fast. For example, a particular doctrine about other religions might be consistent with one central doctrine in the overall scheme of doctrines but conflict (perhaps not obviously) with another. If changing historical circumstances or interaction with other religious communities or other factors brings such inconsistencies to the fore, then decisions will be needed as to whether or not particular doctrines about other religions well and truly express authentic doctrines in a community.

Christian doctrines about other religions have been the focus of considerable discussion and development in recent years as a result of the attention given them at the Second Vatican Council and by the World Council of Churches.

In response to current circumstances of religious interaction, the Second Vatican Council made reassessment of the Catholic community's relations with the main non-Christian religious communities of the world an important item on its agenda. This reassessment produced important conciliar declarations, in which traditional Christian doctrines about other religions figure prominently but in a way that approvingly takes notice of some significant doctrines in each community. Thus the council gave positive accounts of the distinctive answers of Hindu, Muslim, Buddhist, and Judaic communities to fundamental human questions about the meaning of life and the mystery that encompasses it.[5] According these traditions a place in the divine plan of salvation, the council also affirmed confidence in the possibility of the eternal salvation of the adherents of these traditions and in their possession of at least partial religious truth.[6] The council encouraged Christians to recognize that other religions can prepare the way for the acceptance of the truth of the Gospel to which all Christians must bear faithful witness.[7] In addition to these doctrines about other religions, the council also recommended that Catholic Christians engage in dialogue with the members of non-Christian religious communities.[8] This policy has in fact been pursued at an official level since 1964 by the Vatican Secretariat for Non-Christians and was confirmed by the extraordinary synod of bishops held in 1985 to mark the anniversary of the Second Vatican Council.[9]

5. Dogmatic Constitution on the Church, art. 16, *The Documents of Vatican II*, Walter M. Abbott, ed. (New York: Herder and Herder/Association Press, 1966), 34–35.

6. Declaration on the Relationship of the Church to Non-Christian Religions, arts. 1–2 (Abbott, 660–63).

7. Decree on the Church's Missionary Activity, art. 3 (Abbott, 586–87); Dogmatic Constitution on the Church, art. 16 (34–35).

8. Declaration on the Relationship of the Church to Non-Christian Religions, art. 2 (Abbott, 661–63); Pastoral Constitution on the Church in the Modern World, art. 92 (305–6).

9. "The Church in the Word of God Celebrates the Mystery of Christ for the Salvation of the World," Final Report of the 1985 extraordinary session of the Synod of Bishops, section D, art. 5 (*Origins* 19 [1985], 450).

Similar developments have occurred in the World Council of Churches since its fourth assembly at Uppsala in 1968. Uppsala adopted a "Report on Missions" stating in part that dialogue is a "human, personal, relevant and humble" approach to those of other faiths or no faith, which enables us to "share our common humanity" and "express our common concern" without implying "a denial of the uniqueness of Christ."[10] In 1971, the central committee of the WCC established a subunit on Dialogue with Men of Living Faiths and Ideologies. The fifth assembly (Nairobi, 1975) reaffirmed the importance of dialogue in a report that emerged from sectional debate in which positions ranged from fear of "spiritual compromise" (expressed especially by Orthodox and Scandinavian Lutheran churches) to the desire "for a more definite endorsement of the dialogue approach" (expressed especially by Asian churches).[11] In 1979, the central committee adopted "Guidelines on Dialogue."[12] The Vancouver Assembly (1983) affirmed that dialogue is "a mutual venture to bear witness to each other and the world, in relation to different perceptions of ultimate reality."[13]

The doctrinal implications of such initiatives are clear when we consider the significance of the Second Vatican Council's teachings on other religions. These teachings and the policies they warrant can be construed as endeavoring to develop traditional Christian doctrines about other religions in a way that takes account of the distinctive claims advanced by other religious communities. The Council's Declaration on the Relationship of the Church to Non-Christian Religions does this explicitly by taking up in turn the doctrines of the Hindu, Buddhist, Muslim, and Ju-

10. *The Uppsala Report,* edited by Norman Goodall (Geneva: World Council of Churches, 1968), para. 6.

11. *Breaking Barriers, Nairobi, 1975,* edited by David M. Paton (Grand Rapids: Eerdmans, 1976), 70–85.

12. *Guidelines on Dialogue* (Geneva: World Council of Churches, 1979).

13. *Gathered for Life: Official Report of the VI Assembly of the* WCC, edited by David Gill (Grand Rapids: Eerdmans, 1983), 40.

daic communities at least in a general way and approving of the truth and rightness expressed in their beliefs and precepts.[14] The declaration thus teaches some specific doctrines about the doctrines of other religions. As it happens, the doctrines whose truth and rightness it acknowledges turn out to be identical with Christian doctrines. The declaration does not note the truth and rightness of any non-Christian doctrines that the church itself does not teach in some form. Hence the declaration does not state that any strictly alien religious claims are true and right, but neither does it exclude this possibility. The recommendation to engage in dialogue presumably opens this possibility up for further exploration. The council does not address the question of whether it is possible for non-Christian religious doctrines to suggest developments of Christian primary doctrines other than those in which something is taught about other religions.

It seems clear, then, that the Second Vatican Council sets the stage and indeed leads the way for developments in those doctrines about other religions that have become standard across the Christian communities. The potential for such developments arises (logically speaking) when a Christian community takes note of the distinctive doctrines of other religious communities in the course of elaborating doctrines about them. Some such doctrines are found in germ in the conciliar statements. The recommendation to engage in interreligious dialogue at least supposes, even if it does not explicitly envisage, that additional developments along these lines are possible.

The forms of dialogue with which Christians have become familiar—interconfessional dialogue and dialogue with modern thinkers—are in marked contrast to the situation posed by interreligious dialogue. Here, Christian communities confront, not disagreements arising from a fundamentally shared faith or from the critique of secular philosophies, but massive and enduring

14. Declaration on the Relationship of the Church to Non-Christian Religions, arts. 2–4 (Abbott, 661–67).

bodies of religious wisdom and highly ramified systems of doctrines derived from sources as ancient and rich as any of their own. The challenges posed by this encounter come not from religiously skeptical individuals but from religious communities advancing well-developed alternative conceptions of the ultimate aim of life and the pattern life ought to have in view of this aim.

Interreligious dialogue is a form of religious interaction in which members of different religious communities engage in conversation about various features of their distinctive traditions and patterns of life. In line with the wide variety of purposes that might be pursued by conversations of this sort, there would be opportunities for a variety of utterances in such settings. Participants might report about the historical development or subtle meanings of some aspects of their traditions. They might offer examples of their communities' prayers or relate events in the lives of their communities' founders or saints. In addition to employing utterances for these and other purposes, the participants would have occasion to mention some of the doctrines of their communities. Given the seriousness with which they view the conversation and the respect with which they regard the other participants, they would have to be prepared to present some reasons for doctrines that (as persons who profess adherence to particular religious traditions) they hold to express true beliefs and right courses of action. Since there would presumably be disagreements among participants whose communities teach different and possibly conflicting doctrines, those engaged in dialogue would have to acknowledge the distinctiveness of the doctrines presented by other communities represented in the dialogue. Serious recognition of the diversity of religious doctrines would be important at least as an initial state of mind, even if the participants were to conclude at the end of dialogue that the oppositions among their doctrines were only apparent ones and that at some deeper level the doctrines of their different communities were all consistent with one another.

This description of the logical features of interreligious dialogue suggests that the course of action recommended in dialogue policy is a complex one. This recommendation in a Christian community would seem to include at least the following recommendations as well: (1) Christians should respect other dialogue participants both as fellow human beings and as fellow seekers after religious truth; (2) Christians should study and esteem the doctrines of the other religious communities represented in dialogue; (3) Christians engaged in interreligious dialogue should be prepared to propose, develop, and argue for their doctrines; (4) Christians should take notice of the proposals of alien religious claims and the arguments that may be advanced in their behalf by other dialogue participants; (5) Christians should be open to possible developments of their own doctrines that might be suggested in the course of their study of other religions and in dialogue with their adherents. If a religious community teaches its members to engage in dialogue, it must at least envisage the possibility that its members will have occasion to engage in an interreligious dialogue with the features described above. It is reasonable to assume, therefore, that if it commends dialogue, it commends courses of action 1–5 as well. Someone who recommended participation in dialogue might be unaware that in doing so he was by implication recommending other specific courses of action along with it. If for some reason he could not accept one of the implied recommendations, he might decide to withdraw his recommendation to engage in dialogue or at least to rethink the objectionable item in the series. But unless the contrary is explicitly indicated, it is reasonable to assume that in recommending dialogue a religious community recommends as well the courses of action ingredient in it.

In teaching the policy of dialogue, the Catholic community—and Christian communities that accept WCC recommendations—can be regarded as having envisaged the setting of interreligious dialogue as described above. It is reasonable to assume that in recommending that their members engage in dialogue with other religions, Christian communities can be understood to be teaching 1–5 as well. These communities can therefore be taken to suppose 1–5 to be consistent with their other main doctrines about other religions.

At this point, the particular doctrinal commitments of the various Christian communities would come into play in the development of doctrines about other religions consistent with engagement in interreligious dialogue. In order to avoid eliding doctrinal differences among Christian communities, our attention here is focused principally on exploring Catholic approaches to these issues. Presumably this exploration will have some bearing on developments that might be required in the theology of religions of other Christian communities.

The valuations conveyed in traditional Christian doctrines about other religions—as the Catholic community understands them—plainly support the attitudes of respect and esteem supposed by the determination to engage in interreligious dialogue. Faith in God's all-embracing providential care for the human race would seem to require of Christian communities that they admit that their own traditions could not have a monopoly on religious truth and virtue. Charity and justice demand that Christians appreciate the goodness of other religious people; the truth of some of their doctrines about God, the human condition, and other matters; the rectitude of their moral codes; the beauty of their ritual; the wisdom of their institutions; and the marvels of their art, literature, and culture. It seems clear that standard Christian doctrines about other religions could be construed to warrant the respect, esteem, and readiness to study that are commended by recommendations 1 and 2.

This supposition seems to be on equally firm ground with regard to recommendation 3. There is no rule that requires Catholic Christians to remain silent about doctrines of the Christian community in the presence of nonmembers. On the contrary, they are encouraged to bear witness to their convictions and hope about the salvation that God promises. Hence, Christian doctrines can plausibly be supposed to warrant the recommendation that

Christians engaged in dialogue be prepared to propose their doctrines and argue for them in ways that will be comprehensible to persons who do not hold them.

Respect for the possibly divinely inspired truth that may be present in other religions implies a readiness to entertain the doctrinal proposals that may be advanced in the course of dialogue. Nothing in Christian doctrines about other religions can be construed as opposed to taking notice of the alien religious claims that may be expected to be proposed in the course of dialogue. Furthermore, respect for the truth that may be present in other religions implies a readiness to make it one's own. A willingness to appropriate the truths learned in the course of study and dialogue can be shown to be consistent with Christian doctrines about other religions and is in any case well attested by historical precedents.

It follows that the determination to participate in interreligious dialogue opens up the possibility that the theology of religions could develop traditional Christian doctrines about other religions in such a way as to take alien religious claims into account. Doctrines about the availability of salvation to non-Christians and the trustworthiness of their communities to direct them toward it pose an especially difficult challenge for a Christian theology of religions that strives to take other communities' distinctive doctrines about the true aim of life into account.

CHAPTER TWO

Varieties of Religious Aims

"I ONCE READ through a collection of Roman Catholic saints," wrote the Buddhist scholar Edward Conze, "and there was not one of whom a Buddhist could fully approve. This does not mean that they were unworthy people, but that they were bad Buddhists."[1] Conze's remark suggests that the doctrinal standards by which a person would be judged to have attained the true aim of life in the Buddhist community are rather different from those which would be invoked in appraising the whole of a Christian life. Both a Christian saint and a Buddhist *arahant* would be regarded by their respective communities as having attained or being on their way to attaining the true aim of life. Yet the states of mind and being of such persons would have to be described in rather different terms. Seeking, attaining, and enjoying Nirvana are not the same things, Conze implies, as seeking, attaining, and enjoying the perfection of charity or the beatific vision.

Conze thus alerts us to the difficulties besetting a religious community's effort to teach confidently about the chances that outsiders have of attaining the true aim of life, or about the likelihood that their communities actually point them in the right direction and cultivate the knowledge and skills needed to make real progress. The difficulties are compounded in circumstances

1. Edward Conze, "Buddhist Saviors," in *The Savior God*, ed. S. G. F. Brandon (Manchester: Manchester University Press, 1962), 82.

of intense religious interaction, such as our own, when a community's acquaintance with the distinctive teachings of other communities broadens and deepens.

Buddhists, Christians, Jews, Muslims, and Hindus all teach different things, it seems clear, and among the more conspicuous are the different things they teach about the ultimate aim of life and the shape life ought to take in view of this aim. "Nirvana," "Torah holiness," "beatific vision," "submission to Allah," "release from the cycle of rebirth": the major religious communities respectively direct their adherents to final aims of life that seem, at least on the face of things, to differ from one another. These communities foster particular ranges of dispositions in their members, in view of distinctive teachings about the true aim of life, the reasons for pursuing it, and the means of attaining and enjoying it. In varying degrees, each community can be understood to claim that the aim of life it proposes is the one most worthy of pursuit by all human beings without exception. Members of these communities who took part in an interreligious dialogue would presumably be prepared to advance arguments in support of their claims, showing how they were true, right, or good, connecting them with each other in the overall patterns of life they foster, and linking them with other areas of human knowledge and experience.

A religious community that takes its own doctrines seriously would be predisposed to accord a comparable measure of respect to the doctrines of other communities. Thus, in developing its doctrines about other religions, there would be compelling reasons to take the distinctive teachings of other communities into account, particularly as they bear on seeking, attaining, and enjoying the true aim of life.

As we have seen, in the Christian community, doctrines about other religions have arisen largely, though not exclusively, in response to questions about the possibility of salvation for persons and in communities where explicit Christian faith is absent. In current theology of religions, the growing esteem felt by Christians for other religions finds expression in generously optimistic accounts of this possibility. The challenge to blend confidence in this possibility with systematic attention to the varieties of religious aims has proven to be formidable for most theological programs in this field.

CURRENT CHRISTIAN THEOLOGY OF RELIGIONS

Can non-Christians attain salvation? Do other religions aim at salvation? We have seen that some form of the first question has been traditional in Christian theology of religions. The second question has a more contemporary ring to it. Together, these questions consume much of the attention of Christian theologians of religions. So much is this the case that, whatever views they may advance on other issues in Christian theology of religions, rival positions in the field are classified as exclusivist, inclusivist, or pluralist, according to the prevailing typology, chiefly on the basis of the responses their proponents give to these two questions. Like all such typologies, this classification risks caricaturing the positions to which it is applied. As a heuristic device, however, it serves—better than more complicated though more accurate classifications—to identify the chief alternatives in the field, given the centrality accorded by all to the issue of the salvation of non-Christians and the salvific character of their religions.

The esteem that many Christian theologians have come to feel for other religions inclines them to dismiss the exclusivism associated with the notorious formula *extra ecclesiam nulla salus* as offensive to other communities and inconsistent with central Christian doctrines. There is reason to doubt that the formula in its proper use has anything to do with non-Christians at all, for in its origins and subsequent history, this formula was normally lodged as a warning to Christians who broke away from the main body of the church (apostates, schismatics, heretics, and the like). Inclusivist and pluralist theologians nonetheless construe the formula as at least symbolic of the exclusivism they join in repudiating. If we take exclusivism strictly to mean that full salvation (that is, enjoyment of eternal fellowship with the triune God) is in principle attainable only by those who before death embrace an explicit Christian faith and receive baptism, then it seems to be ruled out by a traditional understanding of Christian doctrines as laid out in the preceding chapter. An indication of this is the fact that attempts to extend the formula *extra ecclesiam nulla salus*, without qualification, to apply to non-Christians have been resisted by official doctrinal authorities in the Catholic church. The extent to which any currently influential theological positions merit the label "exclusivist" remains a matter of controversy and need not be decided here. Without seeming to dismiss a set of significant theological positions, however, our concern here is to examine the more widely espoused families of positions represented by inclusivism and pluralism.

Inclusivist and pluralist theologians join in identifying their own positions over against a range of positions viewed by them (accurately or not) as exemplifying the broadly exclusivist viewpoint that ties salvation to the possession of explicit Christian faith. Generally speaking, inclusivists are those who espouse some version of the view that all religious communities implicitly aim at the salvation that the Christian community most adequately commends, or at least that salvation is a present possibility for the members of non-Christian communities. Pluralists contend that all religious communities in effect aim at salvation, but under a variety of scheme-specific descriptions. Although pluralists and inclusivists converge in their repudiation of exclusivism, their descriptions of the nature of the salvation available to non-Christians do not coincide.

When inclusivist theologians assert that non-Christian persons can attain salvation, or that their communities aim at salvation, "salvation" designates all or much of what Christians understand it to comprise: complete well-being in the life to come, in eternal fellowship with the Blessed Trinity and with other human beings, won for us by Jesus Christ through whom grace is given in the present life to nurture the beginnings of this fellowship and to overcome obstacles to its flourishing that arise from creaturely limitations and from sinful actions and dispositions. Christian doctrines about the universal scope of the divine salvific will and the unlimited applicability of Christ's redemptive action are understood to entail that every human being is given the opportunity to attain the fullness of salvation. Inclusivist positions are in recognizable continuity with traditional Christian doctrines about other religions as these were exhibited in the preceding chapter. Their ingenuity in appropriating these doctrines is especially evident in the variety of theories they advance in order to explain not only how non-Christian persons can receive the grace necessary to make this possibility actual in particular instances but also how the religions practiced by these persons can be salvific for them. Theories about the universality of the experience of grace, the possibility of implicit faith, the structure of general revelation, the sources of moral uprightness, and the ubiquity of broadly christological and soteriological motifs figure prominently in the articulation of most inclusivist positions. The burden of inclusivist arguments is to demonstrate that salvation as Christians understand it is in some sense what most religions seek, at least insofar as they express their adherents' grace-endowed present orientation to this aim.

In comparison with inclusivists, pluralist theologians seem to mean something less specific by salvation when they assert that non-Christian persons and communities aim at attaining it. It should be noted that the term "pluralism" can refer either simply to the facts of religious diversity and our heightened awareness of these facts, or to a family of philosophical and theological positions advanced to account for these facts. In the context of the present discussion, theological positions espouse the label "pluralist" in the second sense because of the viewpoint they adopt to account for the facts of religious "pluralism" in the first sense. According to pluralist theologies (and philosophy) of religions, every religious community can be understood to mean by "salvation," at least minimally, a state of being that transcends the limitations of present human existence and that is attainable through the form of life prescribed in the community's teachings. "Salvation" so transcends the human condition as to elude anything but partial description in the limited conceptualities available to religious traditions. Aiming at a strictly transcendent salvation under its various religious descriptions (moksa, nirvana, najat, and so on) is one of the main functions that religious communities fulfill. For Christian theologians who adopt a broadly pluralist reading of the facts of religious diversity, the soteriological core discernible in the teachings of different religious communities warrants a Christian assertion of the availability of salvation beyond the boundaries of the Christian community and independently of the adoption or promotion, even implicitly, of Christian-like practices and beliefs. Here, the dispositions of the universal salvific will of God are taken to entail the divine provision of a variety of parallel or complementary "ways of salvation" in addition to that initiated by Jesus of Nazareth. Pluralist theologians thus construe as "exclusivistic" the traditional Christian claim that salvation—both within and beyond the bounds of the Christian community—is in some sense dependent on the person and work of Jesus Christ. For this reason, in the view of an influential Catholic exponent of this viewpoint, the pluralist program merits the designation "theocentric" to distinguish it from the "christocentrism" of exclusivist and (presumably) inclusivist theological programs.[2]

Inclusivist and pluralist positions respond with strong affirmatives to the questions, Can non-Christians attain salvation? Do other religions aim at salvation? Despite divergent conceptions of what salvation entails, both inclusivist and pluralist positions generally share the assumption that "salvation" is sought by most major and local religious traditions, or at least by their adherents.

2. Paul F. Knitter, *No Other Name?* (Maryknoll: Orbis Books, 1985), 145–204.

Both inclusivist and pluralist positions in varying degrees invoke the empirical study of religions to support their assumption that non-Christians and their communities aim to attain salvation in some form. It can be observed that many religious communities teach something about the human need for a kind of liberation from states of insufficiency variously described as suffering, ignorance, bondage, or sin. In addition, religious communities summon their current and potential members and furnish them the means to strive for a higher state of being in which this liberation will be experienced in combination with many other material and spiritual benefits.

The empirical support for such a viewpoint has become less secure than it was when comparativists sought to employ the category "salvation" to identify certain common features in the doctrines about aims of life among existing (and extinct) religious traditions. More recent comparative work undertaken in this area suggests that earlier studies read a substantial Christian content into the doctrines of other religious traditions. Hence some scholars now seek to construct a definition of salvation that is more widely applicable and less dependent on the specific meanings it is given in the Christian scheme.

Grace Jantzen reflects the more recent view when she remarks that "salvation" even in its non-religious senses is a "slippery notion." She cautions theologians confronted with the rustling world of religions to avoid the unexamined assumption that "all religions have a concept of salvation at all, let alone that they all mean the same thing by it or offer the same way to obtain it: it is misleading to assume that there is some one thing that is obtained when salvation is obtained."[3] For while many religious communities can be observed to teach that a certain present condition of human existence must be escaped or transcended, they differ profoundly in their descriptions of the nature of that condition, of

3. Grace M. Jantzen, "Human Diversity and Salvation in Christ," *Religious Studies* 20 (1984), 579–80.

the higher state of being to be sought, and of the appropriate means to reach it.

Inclusivist and pluralist theologians do not overlook these variations in soteriological doctrines. Indeed, they have developed subtle strategies to encompass them.

Pluralist positions, it might be supposed, would have an advantage here, since they frankly acknowledge the luxuriance of the religious landscape. The proliferation of soterological doctrines in the major communities bears witness to the richness of the fund of religious symbols afforded by human experience of the transcendent. These doctrines should be valued for the exalted conceptions of human life and destiny they embody, and for the ways they complement and enrich each other. Pluralists interpret these doctrines as partial expressions of a commonly sought goal designated by such terms as "Reality-centeredness" (in a currently influential formulation).[4]

Inclusivist theologians take a different tack. Rather than view cross-religious variations as representative of parallel or complementary soteriological programs, inclusivist theologians tend to regard such variations as subsumable into the all-embracing Christian scheme of salvation. The soteriological programs of other communities, despite their apparent variety and barring blatantly corrupt religious forms of expression, in fact hiddenly or partially pursue what the Christian community pursues explicitly and fully, at least insofar as they permit the expression of their members' possible orientation to grace and salvation.

The central concern of much recent Christian theology of religions is thus to allow for the availability of salvation outside the ambit of the Christian community. Despite significant differences, inclusivist and pluralist positions are united in this endeavor. A strong Christian affirmation of this confidence is thought to be an indispensable feature of the esteem that should

4. The term is John Hick's. See, for example, his *Problems of Religious Pluralism* (New York: St. Martin's Press, 1985), 34–45.

characterize Christian regard for other religions and their adherents. In addition, it is argued that acknowledgment of the common quest for salvation supplies the proper basis for interreligious dialogue and the necessary antidote to the exclusivistic intolerance that has given rise to religious persecution and violence.

These advantages notwithstanding, however, there are reasons to doubt that either inclusivist or pluralist positions possess the resources to rise to the challenge posed by current circumstances of religious interaction.

If the argument of the preceding chapter has been persuasive, then it seems that Christian doctrines about other religions should be developed with the characteristic doctrines of other communities clearly in view. Another way of making this point is to say that Christian theology of religions should adopt a doctrinally specific view of religious differences. Thus, with reference to the issues under consideration in this chapter, the availability of salvation outside the embrace of explicit Christian faith should be expressed in ways that respect the distinctiveness and integrity both of the Christian tradition and of the traditions of Hindu, Buddhist, Muslim, and Judaic communities, especially as these bear on the definition of the true aim of life. Esteem for other religions and readiness to engage in dialogue with them presumes at least a forthright acknowledgment of their differences from Christianity and, in addition, a willingness to let these differences count in constructing a theology of religions.

Generally speaking, both inclusivist and pluralist positions appear to be deficient on this score. An indication of this deficiency is that the soteriological doctrines of other religious communities survive their transposition to pluralist and inclusivist theological contexts only with their distinctive features considerably muted. It may be that inclusivist and pluralist strategies for dealing with variations in soteriological doctrines are necessitated by the way the project of theology of religions has come to be conceived. Given the prominence of questions about the salvation of non-

Christians and the salvific value of their religions, most pluralists and some inclusivists are in effect committed from the outset to demonstrating that Hindu, Buddhist, Muslim, Judaic, and other religious communities join the Christian community in the quest for salvation.

The dual specters of exclusivism and relativism presumably exert some pressure on the marked soteriocentrism of typical inclusivist and pluralist positions. If other religions cannot be shown to aim at salvation, then it would seem to follow either that it can be sought and attained only in the Christian community (exclusivism) or, more remotely, that the world's religions are so disparate in their conceptions and purposes as to be without any sort of common ground (relativism). Neither of these outcomes is attractive. Inclusivists and pluralists, despite their differences, are determined to repudiate the arrogant exclusivism that has offended non-Christians in the past. Moreover, they seek a common basis from which to engage in interreligious dialogue and to commit all religious communities to the betterment of the human condition. But the soteriocentrism of theology of religions in this vein seems bound to equalize or absorb the ineffaceably particular soteriological programs of other religious communities.

THE SOTERIOCENTRIC PRINCIPLE

Despite their disagreement on other topics, inclusivist and pluralist positions in varying degrees share the assumption that salvation in some form is what all religious people seek. This assumption has had a long history in Christian doctrines and theology. It is connected with an equally venerable notion according to which Christianity is said to fulfill or supersede other religions. As we saw in chapter 1, contemporary Christian communities inherit these notions from the influential literature in which the first comprehensive account of the relationship of Christianity to other religions was first formulated in late antiquity. In this first theology of religions, the Christian account of other religions was framed largely in the terms developed to describe its relationship to the Judaic community. In much the same way that Christians could argue that the fundamental aim of the Judaic faith was more completely expressed and more reliably fostered by the Christian pattern of life, they sought to show that the basic ethical and soteriological doctrines of the religions and religious philosophies of late antiquity were fulfilled and superseded by Christian doctrines. Indeed, in the continuing debate about these matters between Christians and non-Christians, the central soteriological doctrines of the Christian community underwent important developments. On the basis of the self-descriptions of the adherents of other religious and quasi-religious traditions, Christians could plausibly attribute to these persons the pursuit of the aim of life more surely commended by the Christian community.

The soteriocentric principle may have been a plausible starting point for Christian theology of religions in its origins and much of its subsequent history, but it poses difficulties today in view both of the comparative study of religions and of what other religious people might be expected to say in the course of proposing their doctrines. For one thing, even when comparative study identifies soteriological doctrines in the schemes of other religious communities, it does not follow that they possess the same sort of central significance that doctrines about salvation possess in the Christian scheme. If appeal to the comparative study of religions is to be appropriate in Christian theology of religions, then it will have to be made with the recognition that Christian soteriological doctrines are analogous, not to any and every teaching in other religions about the amelioration of the human lot, but to specific teachings that seek to define and foster pursuit of the true aim of life.

But the more serious difficulty with the soteriocentric principle arises not from the empirical study of other religions but from the self-descriptions of the members of other religious communities. An illustration will serve to make this difficulty more concrete.

Suppose that a Christian theologian should say that Buddhists can attain salvation through the practice of their religion. What was argued by Christians in support of similar assertions in the literature of late antiquity (for example, that Platonists can attain salvation) is assumed to be demonstrable with regard to Theravada Buddhism (and presumably Vedanta, Confucianism, and other religions as well). But in view of what Buddhists might say in the course of proposing their doctrines, it seems odd to assert that their aim is to attain salvation through the pattern of life fostered by their doctrines.

Consider the following statement of some central Theravadin teachings. Like the schemes of other communities, the doctrinal scheme of Theravada Buddhism can be characterized as fostering an overall pattern of life in its members. In this Buddhist scheme there is a doctrine that proposes a comprehensive aim for human life: the whole of life should be directed to the attainment of Nirvana. This practical doctrine recommending a comprehensive course of action is connected with a number of other practical doctrines, summarized as the Excellent Eightfold Path, enjoining a variety of courses of action whose adoption and pursuit are meant to advance one along the way to enlightenment and liberation. In teaching that the aim of life is the state of enlightenment and the extinction of desire, the Theravadin scheme can be said to ascribe an intrinsic value of an unrestricted sort to the state of being designated as Nirvana: it is good without reference to any further object or state of being. Thus, in addition to many practical doctrines, this Buddhist scheme can be said to possess a doctrine that expresses its basic religious valuation. This valuation can take a variety of forms that have in common this logical feature: the ascription of unrestricted primacy-ranking predicates to Nirvana as the state of being supremely worthy of pursuit and attainment.

In the course of explicating the basic religious valuation and the main practical doctrines of this Buddhist scheme, a member of the Theravadin community would probably need to appeal to certain important beliefs about the human condition and life in this world in view of which it is reasonable and proper to seek the aim that Theravada Buddhism recommends for human life. These existential conditions include the various human situations that unavoidably involve unhappiness, the dependent origination of unhappiness in desire leading to successive rebirths, and the need for the extinction of the desire for existence or nonexistence if unhappiness is to cease. Divine or supernatural beings—even if they exist—are subject to the same existential conditions as human beings and cannot be counted upon to contribute to the human advance toward enlightenment.

Much current Christian theology of religions seems to assume the Theravadin doctrine of the extinction of all desire to be in some way analogous to some aspects of the Christian doctrine of salvation, though inclusivists and pluralists would presumably disagree about the nature and significance of this kinship. In any case, the Buddhist account of the true aim of life involves the doctrine of the "no-self": a member of a Buddhist community could be said to have attained Nirvana at the point of realization that there is no substantial or permanent self. The illusion of the self, or the soul, or the inner core of personal identity, must be overcome if true extinction of desire is to be attained. Theravadin Buddhist practical doctrines are intended to bring adherents to this goal.

But for Christian adherents the true aim of life involves continued personal identity—not to mention its fullest possible realization—in a relationship of intersubjective or personal union with the triune God. The practical doctrines of Christian communities are generally intended to foster the development and enrichment of personal life in view of this goal.

It seems clear that significant differences (although not necessarily clear-cut oppositions) obtain between Christian and Theravadin descriptions of the state of one who has achieved the true aim of life. These differences arise from others connected with the basic valuations, the main practical doctrines, and the overall patterns of life proposed in the respective schemes of these two communities. It might be that a Christian theologian well versed in the doctrines and traditions of Buddhist communities could mount arguments to show how these differences could be resolved in particular cases. But in the absence of such arguments it would seem implausible to designate as "salvation" the aims that Christian and Buddhist doctrines recommend and further to suggest that the practical doctrines of these two communities advance their members to the attainment of aims that are in some hidden way congruent or identical. Similar difficulties could presumably be adduced by invoking illustrations from the doctrines of Hindu, Muslim, and Judaic communities.

BEYOND EXCLUSIVISM, INCLUSIVISM, AND PLURALISM

It is not only the soteriocentric principle shared by inclusivists and pluralists but also their respective strategies for accounting for cross-religious variations in soteriological doctrines that cause significant differences between Christian and other religious doctrines about life's true aim to become blurred. This difficulty is more serious for pluralist than for inclusivist positions. Pluralist theology of religions professes to offer an account of the facts of religious diversity that is superior to both exclusivist and inclusivist positions precisely on this score.

Accounting for diversity is less of a problem for inclusivists. In their conception of the issues confronting Christian theology of religions, inclusivist positions are concerned to account not so much for the facts of religious diversity as for the doctrinally required possibility of grace and salvation for non-Christians. This is a traditional concern for Christian theology of religions. In addition, some inclusivists extend traditional doctrine in innovative ways by according a modified salvific role to non-Christian religions. Such positions have the advantage of combining a favorable account of other religious communities with a strong avowal of the traditional Christian doctrine that all salvation comes through Jesus Christ. Inclusivist positions are thus straightforward in their appropriation of classical Christian doctrines about other religions.

But inclusivist positions imply that a non-Christian who is a Buddhist, a Hindu, a Jew, or a Muslim can hiddenly attain salvation in Christ while overtly pursuing the soteriological program commended by his own community. This program may or may not be fully compatible with attaining and enjoying salvation as Christians conceive it, and in any case possesses a finality of its own. Furthermore, by affirming not only that non-Christian persons can attain salvation but also that their communities aim, though haltingly, at salvation as Christians understand it, inclusivist positions tend to sublate the distinctive soteriological programs of other religions in the Christian scheme of salvation. It may be that inclusivists are ready to accept this deficiency as the small price for avoiding the exclusivism that is rightly regarded as being incompatible with historic mainstream forms of Christianity. In the view of many inclusivist theologians, this account adequately serves the intra-Christian purposes for which proposals in theology of religions are chiefly advanced. Such intra-Christian uses do not preclude, inclusivists insist, respect for the distinctive religious doctrines about the true aim of life, even though such doctrines do not come up for direct appraisal in theology of religions in the inclusivist vein.

Pluralist positions merit more detailed attention at this point because they profess to incorporate a more forthright acknowledgment of the diversity of soteriological doctrines. But generally speaking, this acknowledgment turns out to be of little systematic consequence in the articulation of their positions. In fact, pluralist theology of religions tends to homogenize cross-religious variations in doctrines of salvation in the direction of an indeterminate common goal, nonspecific conditions of insufficiency and limitation, and an undefined program for transcending them. What Philip Almond has called pluralism's "principle of soteriological equality"[5] yields an undifferentiated concept of salvation to which no religious community could finally lay claim. Christian doctrines about salvation, no less than those of other communities, are interpreted by pluralist theologians in ways that narrow their scope or blur their distinctive features. Traditional Christian doctrines about other religions undergo a vigorous reconstrual when cast in pluralist terms. In effect, pluralist positions are revisionist in their accounts of both Christian and non-Christian soteriological doctrines. Thus the christological minimalism to which pluralist accounts of Christian soteriology are prone is implicitly paralleled by the pluralist treatment of the particularistic claims to universality of other religious communities as well.

Each of the world's major religious communities seems to combine a claim to the universal applicability of its teachings with an insistence on their privileged and unique embodiment in the community's authentic doctrines. Thus, for example, Buddhists believe that the Dharma—the truth about the way to Nirvana—describes the route for anyone who wants to escape the round of rebirths. Yet, the Buddha is the historically unique "discoverer" of the Dharma. The Dharma is at once universal (in its relevance to the conditions of human existence across time and cultures) and particular (uniquely discerned and taught by Gautama the Buddha). It is only in this perspective that questions about the chances non-Buddhists have of attaining Nirvana are intelligible. Buddhist communities can thus be understood to advance a particularistic claim to universality for what is taught within Buddhism about the way to Nirvana.

As we shall have occasion to observe at greater length in the next chapter, the Christian community possesses a similar kind of claim, centered on the person and work of Jesus Christ. In

5. Philip Almond, "John Hick's Copernican Theology," *Theology* 86 (1983), 36–41, and "Wilfred Cantwell Smith as a Theologian of Religions," *Harvard Theological Review* 76 (1983), 335–42.

Christ's teaching, there is the definitive revelation of the way to salvation. In his passion, death, and resurrection, the salvation of all humankind is accomplished. But the logic of pluralist positions seems to entail that any attempt to secure the Christian community's particularistic claim to universality is to be regarded as exclusivistic. In effect, pluralists visualize the exclusivist-inclusivist-pluralist typology as a trajectory away from exclusivism. Even mild forms of claims advanced for the unique role of Jesus Christ and of the Christian community are construed by pluralists as being exclusivistic.

It is for this reason that the contributions to a recent pluralist anthology, entitled *The Myth of Christian Uniqueness,* are for the most part directed to the task of persuading the Christian community to qualify or withdraw its particularistic claim to universality. In the words of one of the volume's editors, the object of the book is to criticize the "mythological sense" of "uniqueness" embodied in claims to the "unique definitiveness, absoluteness, normativeness, superiority of Christianity in comparison with the other religions of the world."[6] This critique of the Christian community's particularistic claim to universality is understood to be fundamental to the development of a pluralist theology of religions.

In his contribution to the volume, Langdon Gilkey displays a fine sensitivity to the peculiarity of the logic of particularistic claims to universality, although he frames the issues in different terms. Referring to the formidable challenge such claims pose for philosophical and theological reflection, he remarks that "in the face of the parity of religions it is almost impossible at the moment to formulate a theological resolution of the doctrinal dilemmas and contradictions involved. The interplay of absolute and relative—of being a Christian, Jew or Buddhist, and *affirming* that stance, and yet at the same time relativizing that mode of

6. Paul Knitter, "Preface," in *The Myth of Christian Uniqueness,* ed. John Hick and Paul F. Knitter (Maryknoll: Orbis Books, 1987), vii.

existence—both stuns and silences the mind, at least mine."[7] It is clear from this remark and the tenor of the rest of his essay that Professor Gilkey is recommending to members of the Christian, Judaic, Buddhist, and other religious communities that they adopt a revised conception of the scope of their doctrines. According to this new conception, these communities could retain the particularistic element in their understanding of the scope of their doctrines (in Gilkey's terms, by recognizing the relative parity of religions), but would have to abandon the universal element (in Gilkey's terms, their absoluteness).

If Christian communities can be persuaded to withdraw or qualify their particularistic claim to universality, then the issue of the availability of salvation to non-Christians is well on its way to resolution. As we have seen, the fact that each of the world's religious communities can be observed to commend an overall aim of life and a pattern fit for its pursuit has led these theologians to suggest that all religions possess what is called a soteriological structure. It follows then that all religious communities can be interpreted as aiming at salvation under different descriptions and that each community, including Christianity, affords access to it through the diverse patterns of life to which prevailing cultural and historical conditions have given rise.

In his contribution to the *Myth* volume, and more extensively in his other works, John Hick argues that the Christian community must abandon its claim to afford privileged access to salvation. Christian theology of religions must move not only beyond exclusivism (the view that explicit Christian faith is necessary for salvation) but also beyond inclusivism (the view that Christ's redemption is necessary for the salvation of all, even those who do not yet acknowledge him) to embrace pluralism. In his view, "the Christian tradition is now seen as one of a plurality of contexts of salvation." In service of this transition to pluralism, Professor

7. Langdon Gilkey, "Plurality and Its Theological Implications," in *The Myth of Christian Uniqueness,* ed. Hick and Knitter, 47.

Hick discerns beneath "the observable facts" of religious diversity patterns of "individual and social transformation." He asserts that "if we mean by a saint a person who is much further advanced than most of us in the transformation from self-centeredness to Reality-centeredness, then . . . each of the great religious traditions seems, so far as we can tell, to promote this transformation in one form or another to about the same extent." Religious traditions like Christianity are to be appraised, then, not on the basis of their claims to provide sure access to salvation, but on the evidence of their success or failure in fostering individual and social transformation from self-centeredness to Reality-centeredness.[8]

"Reality-centeredness" is thus taken to designate the ultimate aim to which Nirvana, union with the Blessed Trinity, Torah holiness, the garden of delights, and other distinctive religious aims in fact point Buddhists, Christians, Muslims, Jews, and others. According to this representative pluralist account, the Buddhist community's recommendation to seek Nirvana above all else, and the Christian community's recommendation to seek union with the Blessed Trinity can be construed as possessing the underlying structure of a recommendation to overcome self-centeredness in favor of Reality-centeredness. It follows that despite the differences between Buddhist and Christian doctrines about the aim of life and the patterns appropriate to its pursuit, both communities can be understood to be aiming at salvation. The pluralistically expressed aims of life in different religious communities articulate a uniformly soteriological structure and teleology.

In its soteriocentric interpretation of the varieties of religious aims, pluralist theology of religions implies that the distinctive aims of life commended by religious communities partially designate something that can be described only by an ensemble of complementary religious expressions. But that something—

8. John Hick, "The Non-Absoluteness of Christianity," in Hick and Knitter, eds., *The Myth of Christian Uniqueness,* 22–23.

whether it is named "Reality," or "Transcendence," or "Mystery"—never in itself functions as an aim. It can never in itself specify the formation of a particular pattern of life, fit for attaining and enjoying it, except in the vastly generalized sense that seeking it requires the avoidance of self-centeredness. No religiously detailed response is possible to the question, What kind of person does one have to become in order to enjoy Reality-centeredness? This is because Reality never appears in itself, but only in the manifestations it adopts or in the expressions by which it comes to be known in different doctrinal traditions. Thus, in typical pluralist positions, the intrinsic connection between aims of life and patterns of life, which appears to be fundamental to the practical programs of existing religions communities, is loosened. It is made to yield to a generalized and broadly nonpluralistic account of the particular religious doctrines that urge the right conception of the aim of life, the right method for pursuing it, and the appropriate dispositions for attaining and enjoying it.

In order to allow for the availability of salvation outside the confines of the Christian community, pluralists recommend that the Christian community (and by implication other communities as well) revise its particularistic claim to universality by accepting the notion of the parity of religions. Pluralist theology of religions would thus in effect modify rather than actually encompass the existing particularities of religious affirmation. Furthermore, beneath the real diversity in their teachings about the aim and pattern of life, an underlying soteriological structure is posited. According to Professor Hick's proposal and in proposals akin to it, the Christian and other religious communities in the world can be viewed, it might be said, as pluralistically soteriocentric in their doctrines about what constitutes the true aim of life.

It would be desirable, however, for Christian theology of religions to take better account of cross-religious variations in soteriological doctrines than inclusivist and pluralist positions commonly seem equipped to do. Although the differences in soteriological doctrines from one community to the next should not be exaggerated, neither should they be underplayed. It may be taken as an indication of their significance that internal debate about this range of issues has sometimes generated disagreements within the communities themselves, to the point of giving rise to the formation of subcommunities divided along the lines mapped by these disagreements. (Consider, for example, intra-Christian debates about the doctrines of grace and justification.) Cross-religious variations in soteriological concepts and doctrines are likely to prove no less significant than strongly felt internal ones.

It should be possible for the soteriological programs of Judaic, Muslim, Hindu, Buddhist, and other religious communities to retain more of their internal significance when transposed to Christian contexts of discussion. This possibility is at least worth exploring. Such an approach, were it feasible, would have definite advantages in the present climate of religious interaction. Esteem for other religious communities seems to require, as we have repeatedly noticed, that the distinctiveness of their doctrinal claims be taken seriously by Christian theology of religions. In addition, Christian willingness to engage in interreligious dialogue seems to suppose a readiness to grasp the whole scheme of practice and belief that another religious community presents to the world. There is an understandable tendency for Christians to want to voice their esteem for other religious communities by saying that they, after all, set out to accomplish just what Christians set out to accomplish, though they express things differently. But a more appropriate strategy might be to try to determine whether the different modes of expression did not in fact signal importantly different aims. It would be basic to such a strategy to take what Kenneth Surin has called the "intractable otherness" of other religions more at face value.[9]

9. Kenneth Surin, "Towards a 'Materialist' Critique of 'Religious Pluralism': A Polemical Examination of the Discourse of John Hick and Wilfred Cantwell Smith," *Thomist* 53 (1989), 655–73.

One way to begin would be to try to place a religious community's soteriological program within the total framework of its body of doctrines. It is at this point that both inclusivist and pluralist positions seem deficient. Both positions fail to account for the connection between the particular aims of life commended by religious communities and the specific sets of dispositions they foster to promote the attainment and enjoyment of those aims. Thus, in different ways, both inclusivism and pluralism tend to divorce what in most religious traditions are understood to be inseparable. Inclusivist positions imply that the affective and intellectual dispositions fostered by different religious communities in fact promote the attainment and enjoyment, not of the aims of life they commend to their members, but of the aim of life commended by the Christian community. Since for pluralist positions the true aim of life always eludes anything but partial conceptualization and thus can never in itself specify the formation of the dispositions to attain and enjoy it, the particular aims commended by religious communities beckon their members, not finally to the ends they commend, but to the enjoyment of an unnameable reality that transcends them all.

There is ample cause for Christian theology of religions to press at the boundaries set by the terms of the current debate among exclusivists, inclusivists, and pluralists in order to point the way to more promising avenues of study and reflection. Rather than ask whether non-Christians can attain salvation or whether their religions aim at salvation, Christian theology of religions might ask: How do the soteriological programs of other religious communities promote the pursuit and enjoyment of the distinctive overall aims they propose for human life? Questions about salvation would continue on the menu, so to speak, but they would take second place to questions about the varieties of aims proposed by religious communities and the patterns of dispositions and actions they elicit.

RELIGIOUS AIMS AND PATTERNS OF LIFE

Torah, Gospel, Dharma: these terms designate patterns of thinking and acting through which religious communities shape the personal and communal existence of their members and equip them for engagement in the whole range of life's interests and occasions. One way for the Christian theologian to grasp what another religious community undertakes to accomplish is by studying the comprehensive pattern of life it commends in its practical doctrines. In its doctrines and institutions, a religious community fosters not only ways of thinking and belief but also ways of being and acting that encompass the whole of life. The community's soteriological program, should it possess one, will have its meaning within this overall pattern.

The Christian theologian can notice that implicit in the proposal of comprehensive patterns of life are proposals about the aim life ought to have as a whole. Each of the world's religious communities seems to propose an aim of life that is worth seeking above other aims, and usually above all other aims as well, though not necessarily to their exclusion. Union with the Blessed Trinity, holiness in all aspects of life, surrender to Allah, the cessation of desire: these are some of the expressions by which the Christian, Judaic, Muslim, and Buddhist communities can be understood respectively to designate that which should be sought above all else.

Consider the following remark by a scholar of the Judaic community. Rabbi Hayim Halevy Donin has written that "the overall reason given by the Torah for demanding of the Jew that he follow all its laws and regulations" is that Israel will become holy. "Speak to the whole Israelite community and say to them: you shall be holy for I the Lord your God am holy" (Leviticus 19:2). The detail and scope of the law are such as to suffuse every part of human life, to penetrate all its crevices, with holiness.[10]

10. Hayim H. Donin, *To Be A Jew* (New York: Basic Books, 1972), 35.

Notice that there is a dual sense to the "ultimacy" of the aims religious communities commend to their members, and to potential members as well. Ultimate aims elicit comprehensive courses of action, which in turn shape specific courses of action. In this way, ultimate aims are in the first place ingredient in particular courses of action. The finality is intentional rather than temporal. The courses of action—specific and comprehensive—that a community recommends in its practical doctrines derive their character and point from the objects they pursue. Thus, in the form of Judaism described by Rabbi Donin, holiness is ultimate in the sense that, whatever else may be sought, it has primacy. But ultimate aims can also be final in a temporal sense. A religious community may project its members to the enjoyment of a future and possibly permanent state, in which what is sought through the course of earthly existence can be fully realized. We may suppose, for example, that the holiness that is ultimate for the Judaic community should characterize not only each individual occasion of action in life but also the cumulative activity of a completed lifetime.

If the specific and comprehensive courses of action recommended by a community's practical doctrines get their point from the ultimate aim they envisage, the characters of the agents for whom these aims are ultimate are also molded by this activity. The pursuit of overarching religious aims is formative of character. Inculcation of patterns of skills, conduct, and experience seems to be a central feature of the practical programs of most religious communities. The point of this cultivation of a range of "virtues" seems to be that it ensures not only the attainment but also the enjoyment of the end commended by the community. In their practical doctrines, religious communities thus commend not only the means to attain the ultimate end of life, intentionally and temporally, but also the dispositions to enjoy it.

Thus, the patterns of life commended by religious communities may be understood as comprehensive in the sense that they give shape to life as a whole in the light of an ultimate aim of life. In this way, they may be said to foster a web of cognitive and affective dispositions, many of which perdure in that they permit the enjoyment of a temporally final end of life beyond earthly life.

The soteriological program of a religious community arises from its complex of teachings about the aim of life, the shape life ought to take in light of this aim, and the dispositions that will foster its uninterrupted (earthly or transworldly) enjoyment. Clearly, the goal of salvation can be understood only in terms of this complex of teachings. In addition, the community's understanding of the ultimate aim of life in part determines its conception of the potentialities of human beings to attain and enjoy it. No aim can have meaning for persons who are not, or cannot become, in some sense fit to seek and obtain it. Thus, a community's soteriological doctrines normally comprise distinctive conceptions of human nature and the limitations that beset it. Finally, the means by which these limitations are to be transcended are defined by the whole ensemble of the community's practical doctrines.

It seems correct to conclude that the person whom the community could pronounce to be "saved" (to employ a Christian locution) would be a person whose life had been shaped according to the distinctive pattern it fosters. Whether it could judge someone to be saved whose life had not been shaped in this way would be an issue of considerable complexity. Some religious communities, like Christianity, have addressed themselves to it. The issue will be of concern precisely because the pursuit of a particular form of life and the attainment of the aim it promises are linked so inextricably in the ethos and idiom of most religious communities. As we have had occasion to notice, the Christian community is not alone in facing this kind of issue.

The preceding analysis lends support to the theological endeavor to find an alternative to the inclusivist and pluralist assimilation of the soteriological programs of other religious communities. This line of inquiry can be pursued further by making the foregoing analysis more concrete through consideration of some illustrations of the connections between soteriological programs and the comprehensive patterns of life communities commend.

Consider one specific description of the Christian pattern of life. Its formulation is influenced by the Roman Catholic tradition, particularly in its articulation by Thomas Aquinas. Presumably, other Christian traditions could develop comparable descriptions for similarly illustrative purposes. It is presented in order to exhibit more clearly the potential significance for theology of religions of the truth that other religious communities propose distinct (though not necessarily opposed) patterns of life in view of particular definitions of the overall aim of life.

The Christian community can be understood to propose that the most important thing in life is to enjoy a relationship of love, or *caritas,* with the Blessed Trinity. This relationship is initiated by God himself in the sacrament of baptism and fostered through the other sacraments. It is a relationship flowing into all dealings with other human beings, and culminating in beatific vision in the life to come. Beatific vision involves not the static contemplation of the divine essence but a direct knowledge and experience of God's personal life that bursts forth in love. The term "vision" describes the degree of intimacy at the heart of the culmination of the life of charity: it is unmediated, unobstructed, direct love. The term "beatific" describes its blissfulness. It could be said that the fact that interpersonal relationships in *caritas* are fundamental to human existence is confirmed for Christians by the doctrine that relation is found in God himself. The disposition to be drawn into relation with the Blessed Trinity and with others in God is itself God's gift, the infused theological virtue of charity. Everything in Christianity is geared to the cultivation of these relationships in *caritas.*

The formative character of these convictions is clear in the annual observance of the liturgical season of Lent-Easter, from Ash Wednesday through Easter to Pentecost, and by extension to the feast of the Blessed Trinity. Perhaps more explicitly than any other in the liturgical year, this sequence of weeks is devoted to the cultivation of Christian life and virtue, with the primacy of charity as the focal point. The practices of penance and the cultivation of virtue are activities not chiefly self-directed, but oriented to the enablement and enhancement of love for God and others. The more human beings are drawn away from sinful patterns of life through the grace of conversion, the more they are drawn into communion with others and with God.

In Lent the commitment to the struggle against sin is firmly located in "taking up the cross" with Christ. Here, soteriology becomes concrete, so to speak. Through the lectionary ordering and pairing of readings from the Scriptures, as well as through the prayers, prefaces, and hymns, and the evolving liturgical "moods" of this season, the Christian's struggle is continually linked with crucial moments in the narrative of Christ: temptation, transfiguration, cross-bearing, death, resurrection, and glory. The action that once and for all accomplished our salvation now transforms our lives in grace. Our appropriation of the benefits of this action takes many forms over the course of our lifetimes. There is an important sense in which this transformation entails a "conformation." The pattern of the uniquely specifying actions that won our redemption is replicated in the faithful following of Christ by each Christian disciple. When Christ tells his disciples at Caesarea Philippi (Matthew 16:13–28, a passage that plays an important role in linking Christian identity with the narrative of Christ's *passio*) that through him is the way to find one's true identity, he in effect links their transformation with a conformation to him. The *imago dei* is brought to perfection in his disciples by his Holy Spirit, who assimilates them to the perfect image, who is the Son. Thus the community can pray that the Father, according to one of the eucharistic prefaces, "might see and love in us what he sees and loves in Christ."

But conformity to Christ does not involve a finally anonymous uniformity. Rather, Christ's grace unlocks the potential for the realization of the unique personal identity of each disciple. The victory of Easter wins for Christ's disciples the resurrection of the body: the transfigured but perduring personal identities of an indefinite number of uniquely specified, "named," persons. These persons dwell in the perfect union of *caritas* with each other and the Blessed Trinity, itself personally "Named," in the life to come. "And we all, with unveiled faces, beholding the glory of the Lord, are being changed into his likeness from one degree of glory to another" (2 Corinthians 3:18).

It is worthwhile to linger over this description in order to make clear how concretely Christian soteriological doctrines are set into the whole Christian pattern of life. If some such description is persuasive, it suggests that the dispositions to attain and enjoy the true aim of life develop over the course of a lifetime of divinely engendered and sustained "cultivation." Christian salvation means, finally, becoming a certain kind of person, one who can enjoy the end of life that the Christian community commends. It makes no difference to the specificity of this aim that Christians believe it to be identical with the aim all human beings should seek. The single, divinely willed order of grace and salvation, according to Christian doctrines under the construal that informs this discussion, embraces the entire human race. It remains true, nonetheless, that the salvation to which, by God's design for the human race, the Christian community bears witness and affords access comprises a highly specified aim, range of dispositions, and pattern of transformation.

The soteriological programs of other religious communities are likewise embedded in larger contexts of belief and practice. Hence, it is misleading to extract soteriological fragments from the various comprehensive patterns of life commended by other communities in order to show that all of them aim at salvation, because either salvation in some form, or Christian salvation implicitly, is what all religions seek in their doctrines and life.

Earlier we saw that the Theravadin Buddhist community aims at a state in which the impermanence of personal identity would be "realized" and with it the cessation of desire "enjoyed." This Buddhist community would presumably set out to cultivate in its members dispositions that would foster this realization and enjoyment. Also, presumably, these would be different from dispositions, such as those fostered by the Christian community, which have in view the fulfillment of personal identity and the perfection of personal relations. There is reason to suppose that the dispositions to attain and enjoy the perfect fellowship of charity would be different from those needed to attain and enjoy a state of being called Nirvana or enlightenment. Clearly, furthermore, the soteriological program of such a community would be likely to differ from that of Christianity on such issues as the conditions of human existence and the means by which they are to be transcended or transformed.

Suppose that a Buddhist should wish to express confidence about the chances of some Christians' attaining Nirvana. Suppose further that in order to do so he should assert that some Christians attain enlightenment and the final extinction of desire insofar as they find and follow the Excellent Eightfold Path laid out in a hidden way in Christian doctrines. To pursue the illustration further, suppose that a Christian should accept such a statement as a well-intentioned acknowledgment of the religious and ethical values of Christianity on the part of some Buddhist. The Christian might nonetheless be inclined to regard this Buddhist valuation of Christianity as somewhat improbable since Buddhist doctrines and Christian doctrines do not, at least on the face of things, foster the same dispositions or commend the same comprehensive patterns and aims of life. This would be true even if elements of the Excellent Eightfold Path could be isolated in Christian doctrines, especially in practical ones.

The Christian pattern of life is centered on God as the source and term of the fullest possible human realization in eternal life. Hence a Christian might have some difficulty seeing how the doctrines and life of his community foster an aim of life rather different from the one they expressly commend and support. As Theravadin Buddhist doctrines can plausibly be construed to teach, the true aim of life consists not in a permanent intersubjective and personal union with any divine being but in the extinction of desire, and with this the extinction of the desire for personal identity. A Buddhist who wanted to frame his acknowledgment of the worth of Christianity in terms of an ascription of direct contributory value would have to show how particular Christian doctrines advance the attainment of an aim other than the one they explicitly commend. In the absence of arguments showing this, the Buddhist valuation might well seem implausible and irrelevant in view of the dispositions fostered in the Christian community.

A possible pluralist objection to this whole line of argument is germane at this point. It might be objected that neither "Blessed Trinity" nor "enlightenment" properly describe the essentially indescribable "transcendent," but could only aim at describing it. This objection misses the mark. Experientially, it matters little that the expressed objectives do not adequately describe the "transcendent." Whatever the character of the religious conceptions about the aim of life, just as such do they function to specify the dispositions and activities cultivated in view of their present or eventual attainment and enjoyment. To say that religions aim at "ultimacy" or at "reality" is to state an aim of such generality as to fail entirely to describe what actually transpires in religious communities. To be sure, Christians, Jews, Muslims, Hindus, Buddhists, and others not only disagree on how to describe the "ultimate": they disagree profoundly about what the "ultimate" is in itself. But even if it were conceded that these were disagreements only about descriptions of something in itself utterly indescribable, the argument here would still stand. Conceptions of the end of life function as objectives that specify dispositions, activities, and patterns of activity nonetheless.

Do the practical doctrines of the Buddhist community described above commend an aim of life that, in addition to being different from the one proposed by Christianity, is also opposed to it? Are they so opposed that seeking and attaining the one would exclude seeking and attaining the other?

There are at least two ways in which it could be shown that aims of life were opposed: if the courses of action which they recommended were incapable of joint fulfillment, or if the dispositions they undertook to cultivate ruled out or neglected the cultivation of some others. Two aims of action, each having primacy, would be opposed to each other. But distinct aims can be interrelated with, or subordinated to, or independent of, one another. In that case, the pursuit of one aim would not necessarily exclude another. These connections might not be apparent at first. Sometimes, in the pursuit of one aim, an agent unknowingly promotes his attainment of another. One might discover that one had unintentionally developed the potential to be a baseball pitcher by often throwing stones while growing up. Practicing the cello would not contribute directly to developing a marathon runner, but neither would it exclude such an aim. On the other hand, the type of physical conditioning needed to produce a sumo wrestler would presumably rule out a career in the ballet.

Just as in these ordinary human endeavors, there are likewise many possibilities in the religious realm. Extensive comparative analysis and dialogue would be required before doctrinal differences about the true aim of life between Christianity and other religious communities could be identified as true oppositions. After such study and reflection, a Christian theologian might be led to propose, for example, that the pursuit of "enlightenment" was subordinate and not opposed to the pursuit of fellowship with the Blessed Trinity. But the argument here does not hinge on a specification of the nature of the differences that might come to be identified. Rather, it makes a case for the significance of precisely the kinds of analysis at which the foregoing illustrations merely hint. Venturing beyond the conversation that currently engages exclusivists, inclusivists, and pluralists, Christian theology of religions would endeavor to frame its confidence in the availability of salvation beyond the confines of the Christian community in a manner consistent with an acknowledgment of the varieties of aims pursued by other religious communities.

CHAPTER THREE

The Providential Diversity of Religions

THE DHARMA, writes the Mahayana Buddhist scholar Sangharakshita, is not "just one more path to Nirvana, but the underlying principle, the *rationale*, of all paths. . . . Outside the Dharma it is impossible to go, for it presents in their most universal, and hence in their most individual aspect, those teachings which in other religions are more often found in fragmentary and distorted forms."[1] In this connection, Phra Khantipalo suggests that Buddhism's relationship to other religions can be described by saying that "within Buddhism all other religions can be contained accurately. It is thus possible to plot with precision the various levels to which Hinduism, Christianity and Islam rise within the all-embracing thought of the Enlightened One. It is not possible to fit Buddhism into the range of thought of others without distortions, prunings, abuse or persecution." Centuries earlier and with different religions in view, a parallel insistence on the "uniqueness of Buddhism" was expressed by Dogen: "The phrase 'the identity of the three religions' [viz., Buddhism, Taoism, Confucianism] is inferior to the babble of babies. Those who use it are the destroyers of Buddhism."[2]

1. Sangharakshita, *A Survey of Buddhism*, 5th edition (Boulder, Colorado: Shambhala Publications, 1980), 37–38.

2. Phra Khantipalo, *Tolerance: A Study from Buddhist Sources* (London: Rider & Company, 1964), 36–37.

The advisability of maintaining our inquiry on its present course is confirmed by remarks like these. They suggest that there are good reasons to try to steer Christian theology of religions away from its current preoccupation with questions about the salvation of non-Christians and the salvific character of their religions. Perhaps these questions are best handled as a subset of questions about the varieties of aims they pursue. In any case, such remarks invite inclusivists and pluralists to set aside, at least experimentally, the soteriocentric principle when conceiving Christian relations with other communities. We have observed that this principle tends to obscure the distinctive soteriological teachings other traditions propose and with these the overall point of the patterns of life they commend. Buddhists like Khantipalo and Sangharakshita, and religious people generally, find it hard to see how they can be pursuing what Christians understand by salvation.

Some theologians defend the soteriocentric principle by contending that the positions it supports are developed primarily for intra-Christian use. But we have seen that renewed esteem for other communities and the willingness to participate in dialogue with them commits Christian communities (logically speaking) to developing their doctrines about other religions in ways that will do justice to the distinctive teachings of other traditions. In dialogue, distinctive doctrinal claims are advanced as elements of larger bodies or schemes of doctrines in which beliefs, valuations, and practical doctrines would be connected with each other in complex ways. By teaching their members to engage in conversations of this sort, Christian communities suppose that Christian doctrines about other religions could be formulated with attention to Buddhist as well as other religious patterns of life. In this way, theology *for* dialogue furnishes a solid basis for theology *in* dialogue.

In its current forms, Christian theology of religions has been preoccupied with the question, Do other religions aim at salvation? It should be plain that no blanket affirmative response to this question is either possible or appropriate. Judgments about the matter would depend on knowing something rather specific about the doctrines of the religious communities in question, especially their doctrines about life's overall aim and shape. Furthermore, it would have to be clear not only what is meant by "salvation" but also how a soteriological program fits into the larger context of the body of doctrines of a community. In the terms of the analysis offered in the preceding chapter, this question might be better framed: Do other religious communities, while pursuing their distinctive aims, foster rather than obstruct the development in their members of the dispositions to attain and enjoy the true end of life, fellowship with the Blessed Trinity? The Second Vatican Council's Declaration on Non-Christian Religions can be construed as offering a qualified affirmative response to this question, though without framing it in these terms.[3]

While Christians cannot state without qualification that other religious communities aim at salvation, it by no means follows that they can say nothing positive about these communities, or that their members are excluded from sharing fully in salvation. There are other ways of expressing an appreciative valuation of non-Christian religious communities that would be preferable in present circumstances. There are alternatives to asserting that other religions are partially equipped to attain that to which Christianity affords surer success (as in some versions of inclusivism), or that all religions are more or less equally equipped to attain something that finally eludes them all (less satisfactorily, in most versions of pluralism). Christian theology of religions might investigate, according to George Lindbeck, the "unsubstitutable uniqueness of the God-willed missions of non-Christian religions within which potentialities can be actualized and realities explored that are not within the direct purview of the peoples of

3. Declaration on the Relation of the Church to Non-Christian Religions, *The Documents of Vatican II*, ed. Walter M. Abbott (New York: Herder and Herder/Association Press, 1966).

Messianic witness, but are nevertheless God-willed and God-approved anticipations of aspects of the coming kingdom."[4] Once freed of the assumption that other religious communities aim to accomplish the same things that Christianity does, Christian theologians will have much to learn from the study of their literatures as well as from the debate that such study is likely to engender. Given the profundity and scope of these literatures, not to mention their sheer volume, the potential for further theological inquiry and construction is virtually unlimited. In addition, a theological position developed along these lines will conceive and address the issue of the eternal fate of the members of other religious communities in a way that respects the aims of life they now pursue.

DEVELOPMENTS OF CHRISTIAN DOCTRINES ABOUT OTHER RELIGIONS

To gain some perspective on this range of possibilities, consider again the Christian doctrines about other religions sketched earlier:

C1. Other religions teach partial truth in comparison with the fullness of truth taught in the Christian community.

C2. Other religions are superseded by Christianity.

C3. Other religions could play some role in the divine plan of salvation.

C4. Members of other religious communities could be in fellowship with God and thus in some hidden way be members of the Christian community.

C5. Members of other religious communities could possess an implicit faith, which could become explicit in Christianity.

C6. Members of other religious communities could perform good actions having salvific value for them.

4. George A. Lindbeck, *The Nature of Doctrine* (Philadelphia: Westminster Press, 1984), 54.

It was suggested in chapter 1 that these working formulations can function as a handy summary of standard Christian doctrines about other religions as these emerged in the course of centuries of engagement and reflection. What developments of these doctrines might be appropriate in the circumstances defined by the commitment to engage in interreligious dialogue adopted by many Christian communities today?

The following are some possibilities for consideration:

C1* Other religions could teach many true and right doctrines, some of which may be more fully expressed in Christianity.

C2* Other religions are superseded by Christianity as ways of salvation.

C3* Other religions could play a real but as yet perhaps unspecifiable role in the divine plan of salvation to which Christianity bears unique witness.

C4* Members of other religious communities could share in the divinely willed consummation of human history that Jesus Christ makes possible and for which Christians hope.

C5* Members of other religious communities may develop dispositions leading to the attainment and enjoyment of salvation.

C6* Members of other religious communities may lead morally upright lives that orient them to fellowship with God.

Formulations like these ascribe an indirect or providential value to other religious communities without prejudice either to their distinctive doctrines about the aim of life or to the unique valuation of the Christian community entailed by its doctrines about the universality of salvation. In addition, in place of a hidden present affiliation with the Christian community, there is the possibility of a prospective or future fellowship with God and with the Christian community on the part of persons who are now explicit adherents of another religious tradition, or who are not affiliated with any religion.

We have seen that, like many other communities, Christianity teaches that the aim of life it fosters is the one most worthy of pursuit by all human beings without exception. Generally speaking, it has not taught (and in view of its primary doctrines probably could not teach) that salvation constitutes the aim of life only for some limited group of human beings or only during some one segment of the course of world history. On the contrary, as is clear in the historic mainstream forms of Christianity, the Christian scheme is ordinarily understood to include doctrines about the universality of salvation.

According to these doctrines, all human beings who have ever lived, including those who lived before the appearance of the Christian community, are called to participate in a relationship of union with the Triune God. Some Christian theologians have construed these doctrines to mean that the very existence of the universe and of humankind within it is to be attributed in the first place to the divine intention to enter into union with human beings. In addition there is the teaching that human beings, because of both their creatureliness and their sinfulness, could not attain their true and divinely willed destiny without benefit of divine aid. If such is the universal condition, then the divine remedy, to be truly effective, must have a universal impact. Hence the doctrines about the universality of salvation culminate in the teaching that Jesus Christ is the universal savior: human beings who attain their true destiny do so only in virtue of the grace of Christ.

It is doubtful whether a Christian theology of religions could be fully in accord with Christian central doctrines if it taught that the pattern of life and the aim whose pursuit Christians foster were fitted only to particular cultural and social circumstances or only to particular periods in history. A theology of religions that took such a view, as do some pluralist positions, would presumably be committed to the additional view that the different religious traditions that have emerged in various cultures over the course of history each have a legitimate claim to shape the lives mainly of persons who find themselves sharing the presuppositions prevailing in those particular cultural settings. On this account of the matter, the acknowledgment of the diversity of religious aims would in all likelihood include some version of the view that the different aims proposed by various religious communities are each more or less equally worthy of pursuit, depending on historical or social circumstances. But it seems clear that a theology of religions that adopted such views could not be consistent with the traditional Catholic interpretations of central Christian doctrines and particularly of those about the universal scope of the divine plan of salvation.

To assert that other religions could teach many true and right doctrines, some of which may be more fully expressed in Christianity (C1*), respects the distinctiveness of other religious doctrines at the same time that it acknowledges the truth they may express and envisages the possibility that Christians could appropriate this truth. A Christian theology of religions guided by such a formulation of the traditional doctrine avoids the assumption that all religions seek salvation for their adherents. In connection with this, the statement that other religions are superseded by Christianity as ways of salvation (C2*) defines Christianity's overall relationship to other religions rather more cautiously than do either the tradition or its inclusivist interpreters. Taken together, these formulations preserve the unique valuation of the Christian community without sacrificing anything of the specific content of Christian doctrines about salvation or of other communities' doctrines about the aim of life.

These formulations permit a valuation of other religions that is framed in terms of the universal plan of God for the world and humankind (C3*), conveying what may be called an "eschatological" or "providential" valuation of other religions. Instead of ascribing to other religions a present salvific value for their adherents, Christian theology of religions would comprise a valuation the complete nature of which would be disclosed only with the consummation of human history that Christianity longs for and proclaims in its doctrines about the last things. Traditional Christian doctrines about other religions, developed along these lines, can be shown to be reasonably consistent with central Christian doctrines and nonetheless susceptible of plausible specification in statements having as their referents particular religious communities or their adherents—for example:

C1B* Theravada Buddhism teaches many true and right doctrines, some of which are more fully expressed in Christianity.

C2B* Theravada Buddhism plays a real but as yet perhaps incompletely specifiable role in the divine plan of salvation to which Christianity bears unique witness.

In this way, Christian doctrines about other religions *qua* religions permit reference to, although they do not depend upon, what the members of other religious communities might have to say in the course of proposing their doctrines. Such an approach would not forestall the development of Christian doctrines about the doctrines of other communities as further interaction may require. A theology of religions in this vein would be equipped to show that Christian communities' supposition that the policy of dialogue is consistent with their other doctrines about other religions is well founded, particularly in the case of the recommendation to entertain the doctrines of other communities as serious religious alternatives.

The acknowledgment of the providential diversity of religious aims is compatible with a strong Christian affirmation of the universality of salvation. A Christian theology of religions, shaped by this development of traditional doctrines, preserves the unique valuation of the role of the Christian community in the divine plan for humankind. Furthermore, such a theology of religions can acknowledge the distinctiveness and integrity of non-Christian religious schemes and patterns of life. But to suppose that religious communities foster distinctive (as opposed to identical or congruent) aims of life is not equivalent to supposing that the different aims commended by particular religions are all equally worthy of pursuit. For this reason, the Christian theology of religions proposed here would support vigorous defense of Christian doctrines in the setting of interreligious dialogue. The recognition that other communities advance distinctive doctrines with a universal scope does not involve a denial or dilution of Christian doctrines. Rather, it helps to focus more sharply the nature of the encounter between the Christian community and other major religious communities, and the sorts of arguments that are required in the context of interreligious dialogue.

Does this stress on the particular content of the doctrine about salvation have the undesirable consequence of appearing to exclude countless human beings from enjoyment of the promised and hoped-for salvation? A theology of religions taking its cue from the notion of the providential diversity of religions might appear to obstruct one of the very purposes that inquiries in this area are expected to advance. The notion of the providential diversity of religions seems to exclude not only the ascription of a salvific value to other religions but also any real confidence about the present orientation of their adherents to eternal life. This may seem too high a price to pay to gain the otherwise admirable objective of doing justice to what non-Christians might have to say about themselves. Such a theology of religions would do poor justice indeed to what Christians have traditionally thought it necessary to say about them.

In Catholic tradition the chief way of providing for the salvation of non-Christians has been to ascribe to them a hidden fellowship with God and a virtual affiliation with the Christian community on the basis of a Christian valuation of their religious and moral dispositions and conduct. In order to be in accord with traditional doctrines on this matter, a theology of religions would have to include some version of this important set of standard claims.

Generally speaking, inclusivism's ascription to non-Christians of a hidden fellowship with God and an implicit affiliation with the Christian community parallels an ascription of salvific value to their religions. By teaching in its central doctrines that God wills the salvation of all people, the Christian community supposes that its important doctrines about the members of other religious communities could be formulated in such a way as to show how non-Christians could benefit, concretely, from God's will to save them even when they do not explicitly acknowledge him or his loving mercy in their regard. Christianity also supposes that its doctrines about the members of other religious communities could be stated to account for their possible salvation. In addition, by teaching their members to engage in dialogue with other religious people, Christian communities suppose that these doctrines could be developed in ways that would do justice to what other religious people confess in their doctrines and foster in their lives. Can traditional Christian doctrines about the members of other religious communities countenance this kind of development?

Like the valuation developed in which the providential diversity of religions was affirmed (C1*–3*), the phrase "prospective salvation" has the eschatological future in view (C4*–6*). Just as the providential role of non-Christian religions will be fully revealed only when the divine plan has been consummated, so the participation of non-Christian persons in the salvation to come will be sealed by their visible but future fellowship with God and affiliation with the eschatological community of the just. The concept of prospective salvation can also be employed to refer, by way of the theology of death and purgatory, to possibilities in the individual futures of non-Christian persons.

The ascription of a prospective fellowship with God and with the Christian community to non-Christians does not require the support of any properly Christian valuation of their present religious and moral dispositions and conduct. A theology of religions developed along these lines could acknowledge the goodness and uprightness of other religious people without ascribing immediate salvific value to these qualities. Such qualities could be esteemed for the role they play in the pursuit of the distinctive aims of life of the communities of which such persons are members and as the outcome of fidelity to the doctrines, especially the practical ones, by which the lives of such persons in religious communities come to be shaped.

A theology of religions in this vein expresses the presumption that the members of non-Christian communities could give an adequate description—in terms of the basic valuations, practical doctrines, and central beliefs—of the dispositions that are fostered in their communities and exhibited in the conduct of their lives, in their comportment toward others, and in their civic and social intercourse. It would thus be possible to do justice to the doctrines of other communities by acknowledging and respecting the qualities they engender without describing these qualities in primarily Christian terms. At the same time, appropriate Christian valuations of such qualities could be framed in terms of an "eschatological" rather than a present salvific value. The specific ways in which the presently observable and assessable conduct and dispositions of non-Christians will conduce to their future salvation are now hidden from view and known only to God.

THE PARTICULARISTIC UNIVERSALITY OF SALVATION

Embedded in the Christian scheme, and in some other religious schemes as well, is what might be called a particularistic claim to universality. According to traditional Christian doctrines, no theology of religions could be fully consistent with the Christian scheme unless it incorporated some version of the claim that other religions are superseded or fulfilled by Christianity. As we have observed, the standard line of reasoning for this doctrinal claim would appeal to the basic valuation (defining the Trinity as supremely holy and good), the main practical doctrines (commending the true aim of life as union with God), and the central beliefs (especially concerning Jesus Christ and the conditions of human existence) of the Christian scheme. Taken together, these important doctrines entail an ascription of inherent value to the Christian community (where Christ abides in his Spirit) and intrinsic value to participation in its life (which constitutes the first stage in a relationship of union with God). In addition, these doctrines ascribe contributory value to the Christian community, in that it provides the means for its members to attain the full measure of union with God and testifies to the rest of humankind about the nature of its true and divinely promised destiny.

The unique valuation of the Christian community as compared with all other communities follows from these central doctrines. If the true aim of life is salvation as union with God and if membership in the Christian community is the divinely willed means given to attain this aim, then it would not be consistent with central Christian doctrines to ascribe to other religions a value equivalent to that of Christianity. Any acknowledgment of the worth of other religions must be qualified by the ascription of inherent, intrinsic, and contributory value to the Christian community which is ingredient in traditional Christian doctrines about other religions.

An influential inclusivist formulation of this point employs the traditional concept of supersession but departs from its ordinary construal by attaching a temporal qualifier to it. According to Karl Rahner, other religions are superseded by Christianity when (and only when) its message is known and acknowledged by their adherents.[5] Here, supersession (and, presumably, fulfillment) of other religions by Christianity occurs not simply at a single point in the course of universal history but at different points in the particular histories of societies, religions, and individuals. In this way Rahner's theology of religions preserves the unique valuation of the Christian community at the same time that it permits the ascription of a direct contributory value to other religions. For, according to Rahner, Christians ought to appreciate other religions not simply for the possibly true and right doctrines they teach but also for the salvific value they may continue to possess for their

5. Karl Rahner, "Christianity and Non-Christian Religions," *Theological Investigations*, vol. 5 (London: Darton, Longmans & Todd, 1966), 115–34.

adherents even after the coming of Jesus Christ. Rahner's formulation thus gives to other religions a kind of reprieve not usually countenanced by more traditional versions of this doctrine: other religions can be encompassed in God's will to save their adherents insofar as these religions can provide the means by which non-Christians can express their acceptance of God's offer of grace.

But, as we have seen, there are good reasons to doubt the aptness and explanatory efficacy of inclusivist accounts that ascribe direct contributory value to other religions. In effect, such accounts assert that the adherents of other traditions attain through them not the aim defined and fostered by their distinctive patterns of life but that fostered by the Christian pattern of life. Such valuations seem implausible when viewed in the light both of the specific content of the Christian doctrine of salvation and of distinctive doctrines about the aim of life in other communities. Generally speaking, a similar difficulty arises in overly facile formulations of traditional doctrines about other religions that employ the concepts of invalidation, supersession, and fulfillment without qualification.

There is a way to avoid these shortcomings in both traditional and inclusivist versions of the doctrine in question. One could affirm that Christianity supersedes other religions *as ways of salvation*. The inspiration for this suggestion comes from Rahner. The unique valuation of the Christian community is preserved here, but qualified with respect to class rather than, as in Rahner's formulation, with respect to time (or the course of history). That aspect of the particular valuation of the Christian community by which its relationship to other religious communities is defined is framed with respect to the restricted class of "ways of salvation" rather than the universal class of "all religious communities" as in traditional formulations or in Rahner's temporally qualified class of "religious communities which have heard the Christian message." Only to the extent that they can be shown to propose ways of salvation can other religions be said to be superseded and fulfilled by Christianity. The important notion of invalidation is implied here: insofar as they expressly deny that salvation is the true and divinely willed aim of life or propose aims and patterns of life that are clearly corrupt, other religions can be said to be invalidated by Christianity.

An important feature of the alternative being proposed here is that it takes full account of the complex and specific content of Christian doctrines about salvation. This content, as we have repeatedly observed, can be summarized in three basic assertions. First, the divinely willed aim of human life is union with God. Further, the human predicament is such as to preclude the attainment of this aim without divine aid. Last, God intends that Jesus Christ be the unique and unsurpassable source of this aid for the whole human race. These three assertions involve many of the central doctrines of the Christian scheme and are handily summarized by the term "salvation" in Christian teaching, worship, and in many other contexts as well. When the term is employed in Christian theology of religions, it designates something quite specific: the aim of life that is fostered in the Christian community, the existential conditions in view of which it is reasonable and proper to pursue this aim, and the means by which to do so.

The complexity of Christian doctrines about salvation is well illustrated in the liturgical cycle of the Advent-Christmas season in the Catholic community. As is often the case, the concrete setting of liturgical practice serves to illumine the logic of doctrines (or, as the old adage puts it, *lex orandi lex credendi*) and the specificity of the Christian pattern of life.

Thus in the first part of Advent—roughly the first three weeks—prayers, hymns, and scriptural readings focus attention on a future time in the course of human events on this earth when the whole human story will come to its final point, its consummation. Despite present afflictions, Advent worship urges Christians to let their lives be shaped by the hope of full deliverance and of eternal enjoyment of reconciled life in union with the Blessed Trinity and with humankind as a whole. Christian life is to be lived under this promise of personal and universal salvation.

Christian hope in this promise encompasses the eternal life of the members of the Christian community, the final realization of its own special destiny, and the consummation of all of human history. In view of this divine promise, the Advent liturgy commends dispositions of repentance according to which Christians determine not to allow past sin and failure—in their own lives, in the life of the community, and in the life of the world at large—to undermine their capacity to hope for the future.

This message is elaborated in the first part of Advent by a series of lectionary selections from the Bible's prophetic literature, whose original setting was the troubled political and religious history of the people of Israel. But in addition to expressing the promise of a future salvation, these prophecies are taken to refer to the historical appearance of the Messiah. Hence they prepare Christian worshipers for the subtle shift that occurs toward the second part of the Advent season when attention is focused backward to the birth and, by implication, to the story of Jesus Christ. His coming signals the decisive phase in the divine plan of salvation. Now Christians are summoned to dispositions of praise and thanksgiving in view of the salvation already accomplished in the life and destiny of God's only Son. These themes are deftly interwoven in the liturgy of the final days before Christmas in order to proclaim that the Lord who abides with the community of those in the path of salvation is the same one who came to save the world by his life, death, and resurrection, and the same one who is to come again to bring the salvation of the world and the entire human family to its perfect completion. Thus, the season culminates in the feast of the Epiphany, in which the universal scope of salvation is expressly celebrated. In the words of a Christmas carol, "He comes to make his blessings flow / Far as the curse is found."[6]

According to the Christian story of salvation—as it is vividly retold and celebrated during the Advent-Christmas season—God

6. Isaac Watts (1674–1748), "Joy to the World."

has undertaken to bring the larger story of the world to a happy ending. Christians hope for salvation, not because they have learned from experience that things always turn out for the best, nor because they are persuaded that human yearnings for deliverance necessarily entail their final satisfaction. The Christian hope for salvation, in all its aspects, rests on convictions about the reliability of the divine undertakings about which the Christian community is charged to give testimony.

The particularity and complexity of Christian teachings about salvation give force and content to the Christian community's hope that the final consummation of salvation will include the broadest possible range of human beings. Religiously serious persons have sometimes found it paradoxical that the happy ending of the human story as a whole—if there is to be one—is expectantly and, in the Christian view, authoritatively sketched in the story of that particular segment of the human family that has come to be known as the Christian community. There may be paradox but there need be no arrogant exclusivism in this claim. It is no part of the Christian story (at least in its mainstream versions) that only members of the particular Christian community will enjoy the final consummation with which God has promised to end the world's story. It is, however, part of that story that the fulfillment of the divine promise about history's happy ending depends in some largely obscure way on the continued existence of a particular community, limited in duration and extent, within the larger human family. The perseverance of the Christian community in fidelity to its Lord and in persistent narration of its special story is of intrinsic significance for the salvation of the rest of humankind, including that portion of it that existed before the time of Christ.

Naturally, the term "salvation" has numerous uses outside the Christian scheme. Naturally, also, in some of the doctrinal schemes of other religious communities there may be themes that resemble and even restate elements of the Christian doctrine of salvation. The presence of such elements would be relevant to the

Christian theology of religions in the following way. A particular religion could be said to be wholly fulfilled by Christianity if its intrinsic aim could be realized completely by Christianity. Its doctrines about the aim of life would presumably correspond at many significant points with the Christian doctrine about salvation. There might be convergences on such important matters as the basic valuations and beliefs of the schemes of this community and the Christian community. In a similar way, a particular religion could be said to be superseded by Christianity if it could be shown that Christianity does better or more adequately what it seeks to do in fostering its distinctive pattern of life. Perhaps, on the basis of significant resemblances between their doctrines about the aim of life and Christian doctrines about salvation, it would be appropriate in such cases to describe these religions as proposing "ways of salvation."

Thus the phrase "ways of salvation" does not refer indiscriminately to any goal of human aspiration that can be imagined, nor to any means of human amelioration that can be envisaged or ventured within or beyond religious communities. If other religious communities can be shown to foster aims and patterns of life sufficiently distinct in comparison with the Christian view of such matters, then it would be clearly inappropriate to speak of their being fulfilled or superseded by Christianity. It is a conspicuous feature of religious traditions generally that they propose distinctive aims for human life and different assessments of the prospects of human beings' attaining these aims. In certain circumstances—where there are clearly recognizable affinities between Christian doctrines and the doctrines of some other traditions—it might be appropriate to speak of another religion as being corrected or invalidated by Christianity. But even where strands of soteriological doctrines resembling Christian teachings are thought to exist, they may not possess the same central significance in the total doctrinal fabric of the religion in question as they possess in Christianity. In such cases, it would be inappropriate to define the relationship of the Christian community to this or other communities in terms of traditional versions of the unique valuation of the Christian community. The affirmation that Christianity supersedes other religions *as ways of salvation* takes full account of the specific and complex content of the Christian doctrines about salvation at the same time that it incorporates an acknowledgment of the varieties of aims fostered by religious communities other than Christianity.

RELIGIOUS TRUTH AND ITS SOURCES

Christian doctrines about other religions *qua* religions are concerned not only with the availability of salvation in other communities but also with the possibility of truth and rightness in their doctrines. We have seen that, typically, Christians have been confident about this possibility. Occasions for judging whether in particular instances truth can be found in extra-Christian forms of religious expression arise in the course of interreligious dialogue when the members of other communities assert their beliefs or recommend their practices. But, whether or not such occasions arise, teaching the possibility and accounting for it are important functions of Christian doctrines about other religions.

At issue in Christian doctrines about other religions *qua* religions are the sources of the potential truth that may be found in the communal forms of religious expression of other traditions. The interior states of the adherents of other religions (Is their knowledge correct? Do they have implicit faith?) are only indirectly at issue here and will be considered later in this chapter when Christian doctrines about other religious people are discussed.

Varieties of theories have been developed to account for the possibility of truth in extra-Christian forms of religious expression. In general, such theories depend upon an extended use of the Christian doctrine of revelation. Normally, accounts of the sources of the truth and rightness of the doctrines of other religious communities parallel accounts of the truth and rightness of

Christian doctrines. The concept of "general revelation" thus serves to warrant the possibility of extra-Christian truth in much the same way that the concept of "special revelation" guarantees intra-Christian truth.

But there are good reasons to search for alternatives to recent accounts that employ the concept of general revelation to allow for the possibility of truth in the doctrines of other religious communities. In articulating Christian confidence in this possibility, it would be desirable to take a doctrinally specific view of the ways that religious communities, including Christianity, account for the sources of the truth of their doctrines.

The Christian community affirms that it is God himself who invites all human beings to seek, attain, and enjoy the aim of life it commends. However this aim is described (union with the Blessed Trinity or beatific vision), it is understood to be the "true" aim of life on the basis of God's very own promises. Christian doctrines affirm, in addition, that the full nature of the human person appears only in the light of this promise. Christianity's particularistic claim to universality comprises not only a doctrine about the means of salvation but also a doctrine about the knowledge and promise of salvation.

"Beloved, we are God's children; now it does not yet appear what we shall be, but we know that when he appears we shall be like him, for we shall see him as he is" (1 John 3:2). This striking passage from the First Letter of John proclaims a promise about human destiny and furnishes a description of human existence viewed in the light of that destiny. Within the argument of the letter as a whole, it is clear that this promise is part of a larger "message" received from Christ and now proclaimed to others (see 1 John 1:1–5). Human beings who in faith accept this message and the fellowship it entails are now transformed into a new state of being ("children of God"), which both partly reveals and partly conceals a future and more perfect condition of complete union and vision. By faith now, they can be intimately united with God through Christ and in Spirit. In the future, this union will be consummated and the human transformation will be complete.

The logic of the argument of the First Letter of John, and indeed of the Scriptures as a whole, clearly supposes, even when it does not explicitly affirm, that knowledge of the possibility and conditions of this destiny comes from God himself. It constitutes part of the content of a promise. Christian doctrines assert that knowledge of this promise is not, and could not be, the outcome of human discovery and observation. The point of the doctrine of revelation is to affirm this truth about the promise. However optimistic the Scriptures may be about the possibilities of knowledge of God as "cause of the world," it is only by revelation, in contrast with discovery, that we have knowledge of God's self-descriptions and of his promises in our regard.

In this sense, the promise of revelation establishes a domain of knowledge and a perspective on all other domains of knowledge and experience. This knowledge is not opposed or alien to human nature and experience, but neither is it virtually contained in it. Knowledge of the promise has universal relevance in that it both appropriates and corrects other knowledge, especially where the divine identity and purposes, and human nature and destiny are concerned. But knowledge of the promise is ineradicably particular insofar as it is transmitted in sources entrusted by God to the Christian community.

As we have seen, true universalism requires fidelity to the particularities of Christian revelation and existence. There is nothing odd about this. If in his gracious will God intends to enter into communication and interpersonal relations, how else than according to the structures and processes of communication embedded in the makeup of human beings? A presumption here is that, having created human beings to be the sort of beings they are, God binds himself, as it were, to the created structures and processes that he himself established. He shapes his action according to human nature, not overturning the telos of natural processes but acting in a way fitted to the structures of that which he has created.

God squeezes himself, so to speak, into a particular historical trajectory. This does not mean that he limits himself to it, drawing himself up into an obscure corner of humankind. Rather he makes himself accessible in precisely the modalities in which persons become accessible to each other—specifiably, identifiably, bodily, personally—with names, with ancestors, in the context of particular natural and ethnic identities, with particular family ties, and so on. Far from being preposterous, it makes perfect sense—granted, of course, that God's existence is not doubted and the possibility of his being engaged with human beings is not discounted. It makes sense that, if he wants to communicate with us and be intimately related with us, he will do so in the ways by which we become engaged with other persons.

Knowledge of the universal scope of God's saving plan is based on the knowledge that he has acted in a particular way through Jesus of Nazareth. We are aware of God's intention to make himself known to the whole human race because he has revealed this intention in Jesus Christ. Christian confidence that the salvation wrought by Christ is intended for all human beings is based in the knowledge that it has begun with a particular group within the human race. God does not limit himself to a particular culture or tribe, but seeks by this means to have the occasion to reach the whole human race. He makes himself personally known and personally knowable—not simply as the omnipresent power that maintains all things in existence, nor as the cause of the world. Rather, he reveals himself as the personally present agent, speaker, lover who invites the other agents, speakers, and lovers who are his creatures to enter into personal relationship with him and with each other in him. Through an historically identifiable community of persons, God continues to reach out to the widest range of the human race to proclaim the universal scope of his promise.

When used in an array of Christian contexts (catechetical, liturgical, theological), the term "revelation" designates primarily the content, the truthfulness, and the engagement that the promise of present and future union with God entails. The content is the promise itself, combined with divine self-descriptions, an account of human nature and its destiny, the conditions relevant to seeking the true aim of life, and so on. The truth of this content is understood to point to and be guaranteed by the Truth of God himself. When the Christian community proposes something to be believed, or undertaken, or valued in a certain way, it assumes that what it teaches is true, right, and good on God's authority, and that its doctrines are proposed and accepted by its members under this description. Finally, revelation bespeaks the divine engagement into which human beings are drawn. Christian life in all its complexity is oriented to the God who reveals himself in gracious love to be the source and true aim of life for human beings. Christian dispositions and conduct are shaped and supported by God's personal (and not merely causal) presence to his people in love and mercy.

In its primary use, the doctrine of revelation thus functions to designate precisely what is specific to the Christian scheme as it commends the true (divinely revealed) aim of life and fosters a pattern of life fitted to seeking, attaining, and enjoying it. Extending the doctrine of revelation, traditional Christian theology of religions has employed the concept of "general revelation" in order to attribute to divine agency the presumably widespread dispersion of true and wholesome teachings in other religious communities. Talk of "general revelation" is extended and analogous in that the concept of revelation in its more straightforward sense involves a level and comprehensiveness of communication and vehicles of transmission that are lacking outside of revelation properly so-called.

Generally speaking, current forms of theology of religions employing the concept of general or universal revelation are ill-equipped to take a doctrinally specific view of the ways that religious communities (including Christianity itself) account for the sources of the truth and wholesomeness of their doctrines. Perhaps their reliance upon generalized accounts of the sources of religious truth, framed in terms of the formidably unwieldy notion of "religious experience," leads many Christian theologians of religions to miss the significance of these particularities.

Inclusivist and pluralist positions deploy a variety of theological and philosophical conceptualities to explain how "religious experience" provides the required universal access to revelation and how the assorted forms of religious expression diversely articulate this experience of the transcendent realm. The most influential and well-developed inclusivist positions rely on notions of the ubiquitous experience of grace—broadly interpreted in terms of transcendental philosophy—to account both for the privileged access to truth in the Christian community and for the partial access to truth in other communities. While pluralist positions are generally both more philosophically eclectic and theologically revisionist, they converge in ascribing to religious experience the fundamental role in generating equivalently partial religious conceptions of the elusive truth of the transcendent realm.

In the perspective of this book, accounts of the sources of religious truth framed in the combined terms of general revelation and religious experience obscure important scheme-specific particularities in the ways that religious communities identify and authenticate their doctrines.

Current theological positions that employ the concept of general revelation do not always avoid the misleading suggestion that revelation properly so-called occurs in two more or less equivalent forms, designated general (or natural) and special (or Christian) revelation. The logic of pluralist positions really cannot rule out an indefinite number of revelations. Inclusivism retains a more traditional reading of the distinction, which at least accords a certain primacy to special revelation. Such views tend to obscure both the logic of the concept of revelation and the doctrinal warrants for affirming the possibility of truth in the teachings of other communities. As we have already seen, the logic of the concept supposes that "special revelation" constitutes revelation properly speaking and warrants the extended subsidiary use of the concept to describe God's activity in making himself known through his creation. When the doctrine of revelation is taken to encompass both the knowledge of God gained through religious experience, broadly taken, and the knowledge of God and his promises that is his gift to humankind in Christ, then the universal becomes the ground of the particular. In fact, according to the logic of the Christian scheme, the reverse is the case: the condition for the universal dispensation is established in the particular, in the life and work of Jesus Christ.

There is nothing about claims to have undergone religious experience or claims that such experience is endemic to human life in the world that necessarily excludes Christian confidence in the possibility and reality of a divine communication in an historically specifiable and unsurpassable modality. Nor is there any precisely theological problem with claiming that different religions diversely conceptualize experiences of God embodied in the originary and founding events at their beginnings. From the Christian point of view, difficulties arise when a status is claimed for these experiences that is equivalent to that accorded to the self-identifying communication made by God through Abraham, Moses, the prophets, and definitively through Jesus Christ and the apostles.

In addition, the Christian account of the potential truth of extra-Christian forms of religious expression should do justice to what other communities have to say about the sources of the truth of their doctrines. Other religious communities also have doctrines, analogous to the doctrine of revelation, by which the specific overall content, the claim to truth, and contributory value of their doctrinal schemes are designated. Depending on the distinctive features of the logic of their doctrines, concepts like "revelation" and "religious experience" may or may not be appropriate to describe the initial conceptions to which their schemes are a response, or the assumption about the truth of their doctrines that their schemes imply, or the ultimate aims of life that their communities foster. Buddhist doctrines, for example, regard Gautama the Buddha as the rediscoverer of the universal Dharma and stress the role of his personal experience and inquiry, rather than any revelation, in his coming to enlightenment and leading others to it. It seems especially inappropriate to suggest that Buddhist and other similarly nontheistic communities are in fact in possession of some revelation imparted by a transcendent divine agent.

Thus, there are good reasons to seek a different way of allowing for the possibility of extra-Christian truth than is afforded by the concepts of general revelation and religious experience. When Christians want to acknowledge the truth and rectitude that they find expressed in the doctrines and life of other religious communities, they naturally want to ascribe such qualities to God's influence and inspiration. We have seen that Christian doctrines require this. Truth, wherever it occurs, derives from the one source of truth. Still, perhaps full-blown theories of general revelation and religious experience should yield to a more modestly stated affirmation of the ubiquity of divine inspiration in giving rise to truth in religious matters. The sources of the truth and rectitude that Christians want to acknowledge in other religious traditions can be identified as divine inspiration without appeal to theories of extra-Christian, universal revelation that minimize the particularities of Christian and non-Christian doctrines about these matters. There is ample scope then for judgments about the truth of the individual doctrines of other religious communities as these are studied in their literatures or entertained in the course of dialogue with their members.

PROVIDENTIAL ROLES FOR OTHER RELIGIONS

The unique valuation of the Christian community and of its particular role in divine providence does not preclude the attribution to other communities of some role in God's plan for the salvation of the world. Although the providential roles of other religions are less concretely specifiable than that of Christianity (and, as we shall see, of Judaism), it is nonetheless possible to ascribe such a role to other religions without prejudice to central Christian doctrines or to the particular valuation of the Christian community. The notion that other religions play some part in the divine plan accords with traditional Christian doctrines about other religions, in which it has been affirmed that they contribute to the acceptance of the Christian faith on the part of certain individuals or in certain cultures, or that they foster the development of a social climate supportive of values of which Christians approve, or that they may be the instruments of some divine purpose.

In inclusivist and pluralist theologies of religions, this providential role is given a quite specific content: Other religions can play a salvific role in the lives of the human beings who are their adherents. Such accounts ascribe a direct contributory value to other religions in that they view other religious communities as promoting the attainment of the aim of life fostered by the Christian community (inclusivism) or of an aim of life beyond the particular conceptualities of all communities (pluralism). As we have seen, there are good reasons to prefer alternative formulations of traditional Christian doctrines about other religions *qua* religions that better acknowledge the possibility of truth and rectitude in other religions, and that ascribe an indirect contributory (broadly providential rather than specifically salvific) value to them. Such formulations are preferable if Christian theology of religions is to do justice to what other religious people confess in their doctrines and foster in their lives. It cannot in the end be truly respectful of the doctrines and lives of the members of other religious communities to attribute to them the unwitting pursuit of the aim of life as one defines it in one's own community.

We have had occasion to observe that Christian doctrines about other religions have been, and continue to be, profoundly influenced by formulations in which the Christian community explicates its relationship to Judaism. The Christian conception of this relationship has lately been undergoing revision. One important trend in this developing discussion is represented by the effort on the part of some Christians to be more explicit about the permanent providential role of the Jewish community in bringing about the consummation of history. To be sure, the Christian stake in such efforts is considerable: If the promises to Abraham and Moses have lost their validity, then Christian confidence in God's promises in Christ is likely to seem misplaced. But despite the singular importance that Christians attach to ascriptions of providential value to the Jewish community, it is possible that an analogous valuation would be in order with respect to other religious communities as well. The notion of the providential diversity of religions has a valuation of this sort in view.

Once it is clear that a Catholic theology of religions can affirm the distinctiveness of the aims fostered by other religions without prejudice to an affirmation of the unique valuation of the Christian community or of its doctrines about salvation, then it becomes possible to assert that God wills that other religions perform functions in his plan for humankind that are now only dimly perceived and that will be fully disclosed in the consummation of history for which Christians long. Accordingly, other religions are to be valued by Christians, not because they are channels of grace or means of salvation for their adherents, but because they play a real but as yet perhaps not fully specifiable role in the divine plan to which the Christian community bears witness.

This formulation is in part inspired by Rahner's theology of religions, which acknowledges the continued legitimacy of other religions beyond the time of the coming of Christ.[7] An extended legitimacy of this sort implies that other religions can be regarded

7. Karl Rahner, "Christian and Non-Christian Religions," *Theological Investigations*, vol. 5, 118–21.

as encompassed within the divine plan of salvation. This role can be understood to be a providential one (indirectly contributory) though not a salvific (directly contributory) one. It is possible in this context to speak of what might be called the "unsubstitutableness of the God-willed missions" of non-Christian religions.[8]

The providential roles or divinely willed missions of other religions might include the function of teaching some truths to the Christian community. Although Christian theology of religions in this vein precludes the ascription of direct contributory value to other religions, it permits the recognition of the possible truth and rectitude that might be enshrined in the doctrines of other religious communities, whose existence and purposes are, after all, in some sense said to be divinely willed. There is the presumption, then, that Christians might be in a position to learn something from the truths expressed or the recommendations conveyed by the doctrines of other religious communities.

Thus, in the case of doctrines about the aim of life, for example, Christians could discover elements of the doctrine of salvation in religious traditions with manifest affinities to the Christian scheme. On the other hand, it would also be possible for Christians to learn something from religious traditions, like Buddhism, that possess quite distinctive doctrines about the aim of life and related matters. Perhaps Christians will have something to learn from characteristic doctrines of the Buddhist community concerning selflessness, mindfulness, discipline, nonharming relations with subhuman species, harmony with nature, and religious tolerance. Perhaps such possibilities are encompassed by divine providence. There would be many other possibilities here, as many as the variety of religious doctrines in particular communities.

We have already seen that the Second Vatican Council acknowledged the truth of doctrines in other communities as bear-

8. George Lindbeck, *The Nature of Doctrine*, 54.

ing correctly on certain aspects of salvation. In effect, the council recognized the truth of other religious doctrines as truth the Christian community already teaches. But there does not seem to be any reason why the Christian community could not acknowledge the truth of doctrines that it does not itself teach. Certainly, the Christian community acknowledges the truth of, though it does not undertake to teach, many truths in the physical, biological, and social sciences. In addition, there are many examples of permitted theological opinions whose truth, or at least absence of error, the Christian community acknowledges without adopting them as communal norms. Before 1954, the bodily assumption of the Blessed Virgin was a widely held teaching of this kind. The Catholic Christian community continues to permit the Jesuits and the Dominicans their differing theological accounts of the doctrine of grace. These examples suggest that the Christian community might acknowledge the truth of doctrines in other religious communities without adopting these teachings as its own and without prejudice to its own conviction about the completeness of revelation as it bears on seeking, attaining, and enjoying salvation. Thus, there is no prima facie reason why individual Christians might not learn something from the study of Buddhist meditation methods, neo-Hindu conceptions of nonviolent resistance, and so on. If doctrines about these and other matters were not incompatible with Christian doctrines and if they were educible without the adoption of the entire doctrinal scheme of another community, there would be no reason why the Christian community would have to disallow such learning.

The ascription of potentially providential roles to other religious communities would permit Christian theology of religions to propose doctrines about other religions *qua* religions that were consistent with central Christian doctrines (especially those concerning salvation) and that acknowledged the diversity of religions as in part divinely willed. Such an approach reinforces the capacity of Christian theology of religions to do justice to the distinctive doctrinal claims put forward by non-Christian religious traditions and hence its ability to embrace the Catholic teaching that recommends participation in interreligious dialogue.

PROSPECTIVE SALVATION

Can non-Christians attain salvation? The conviction that they can, as we have seen, remains an unexpungeable feature of Christian confession. Mainstream Christian communities have for the most part been confident that, through the grace of God, persons can receive and develop the dispositions conducive to and necessary for the enjoyment of the true aim of life. They can do so even independently of membership in the Christian community, which devotes itself explicitly to the cultivation of such dispositions. This confidence is based on the doctrines of the unrestricted scope of the divine salvific will and the universality of the redemption won for humankind by Jesus Christ.

Once the well-trodden paths of inclusivism and pluralism are left behind, can this confidence find any satisfactory theological formulation? Is it possible, in other words, to account theologically for the availability of salvation to non-Christians without ascribing to them the pursuit of an aim of life that they either explicitly reject or could not recognize as their own? Can Christian theology of religions express confidence that the members of Judaic, Muslim, Hindu, Buddhist, and other religious communities can (now or eventually) attain and enjoy fellowship with the Blessed Trinity while possessing alternative conceptions of the aim of life and cultivating dispositions consistent with these conceptions?

To gain a perspective on this issue, consider the situation of a person who belongs to what Christians would regard as a thoroughly corrupt religion—one, let us say, that centers upon a demonic deity worshiped by rites of human sacrifice. Suppose further that, responsive to the prompting of divine grace, such a person has recognized and distanced herself from the corrupt elements in her religion. Clearly, although Christians might find nothing in this religious community that could be judged to be conducive to salvation, a person who was a member of this community could still attain salvation.

The point of this illustration is certainly not that most other religions are in some way corrupt. Rather, it suggests in the first place that the question of whether non-Christians can attain salvation is at least distinguishable from the question of whether their religions aim at salvation as Christians mean it. Christian confidence in the salvation of other religious people is logically independent of judgments about the aims of life commended by their communities. A blanket affirmation that other religions aim at salvation (in some way or other) is not required to sustain Christian confidence in the availability of salvation to non-Christians. Theological expression of such confidence is consistent with a systematic acknowledgment of the varieties of aims religious communities pursue.

Second, once drawn, this distinction has the advantage of steering Christian theology of religions toward the desired affirmation of the possibility of salvation for non-Christians, but framed with their explicit religious aims in view. It is suggested that this possibility should be considered a prospective rather than a present one.

Moral Uprightness

By recommending that its members engage in dialogue with the members of other religious communities the Christian community supposes that its important doctrines about them could be stated in ways that would do justice not only to what they believe and value but to the way they live. What is most "public" about religious communities is the impact of their practical doctrines on the shape of the lives of their members. This should not be surprising. Most religious communities are concerned to foster patterns of life in their members. Sound doctrine—religious people are inclined to say—is not an acceptable substitute for an upright life. In any case, practical doctrines are a significant part of the heritage of religious traditions and come close to the heart of what they are about. Hence Christian theology of religions should strive to do justice to the practical doctrines and the overall patterns of life fostered by those doctrines in non-Christian religious communities.

Christian theology of religions in the prospective vein affirms that the members of other religious communities could lead morally upright lives that orient them to fellowship with God. This approach is preferable to affirming the specifically salvific character of the morally righteous and altruistic lives of non-Christian persons (as inclusivists generally do). But it would be desirable for Christian theology of religions to avoid the implication that Christian practical doctrines provide a better account of what other religious people are actually up to than do the practical doctrines taught in their own communities. This does not mean that Christians should not *argue* (in dialogue or similar settings) for the rightness of the courses of action recommended by their own practical doctrines. Nor does it exclude the possibility that Christians could acknowledge affinities between elements of other religious patterns and the Christian pattern of life. There are likely to be many such affinities. Rather, a theology of religions in a prospective vein would give primacy to scheme-specific descriptions of the conduct and dispositions cultivated in other communities. In the course of pursuing their distinctive patterns of life, the members of other religious communities exhibit conduct and dispositions that are pleasing to God and that orient them to fellowship with him. Christian doctrines about the members of other religious communities would thus be concerned to express a Christian valuation of their states that would take not only Christian but their own communities' practical doctrines into account.

Aquinas's approach to the issue continues to be viable. Echoing the first chapter of Paul's Letter to the Romans, his approach to the issues of moral uprightness invokes the ubiquity and significance of the conditions for moral choice. Thus, throughout his writings, Aquinas advanced a cumulatively compelling case for the view that every occasion of action poses for each human being the possibility of choosing the moral good and thereby orienting oneself to the ultimate good. Indeed, the consequences of the failure to do so can on occasion be reversed by subsequent good actions. This is the case not primarily because of virtualities present in the conditions of moral action—and not despite them, either—but because of God's grace. Without reviewing here all the premises upon which Aquinas could draw in support of this contention, the point is that he articulates the unrestricted range of the divine action in prompting and rewarding the uprightness of moral choices made by human beings, Christian and non-Christian alike. The choice of the particular, real human good (for Aquinas, the choice of the moral good) is always a confirmation of the human orientation toward enjoyment of the fullness of goodness in God. In the concrete order of salvation, there is no such thing as moral goodness—or moral defect, for that matter—as an ingredient of a purely natural order of things apart from grace.[9] Whether grace is given in baptism or in the "desire" for it, human beings stand equally in the sight of God before their moral choices, despite the many variables (cultural or religious) that may characterize their particular situation and condition.

Plainly, the moral good that in every instance beckons human choice need not be framed in the terms of explicitly religious conceptualities. This view permits a modestly expressed confidence in the possibility that non-Christians would be oriented toward fellowship with God by the morally upright lives enjoined by their specific religious commitments.

9. Thomas Aquinas, *Summa theologiae*, 1a2ae, 89, 6. See Thomas C. O'Brien, "Question 89, 6: A Commentary," in Thomas Aquinas, *Summa Theologiae*, Blackfriars edition (New York: McGraw-Hill, and London: Eyre & Spottiswoode, 1974), vol. 27, 125–33.

Implicit Faith

It is significant that elsewhere, when addressing the question of the faith needed for salvation, Aquinas can be construed as being more cautious in his assessment of the possibilities of salvation for non-Christians, whose explicit knowledge of the faith would of necessity be deficient.[10] It is not important for our purposes to identify the explicit content Aquinas stipulates as necessary for salvation (in fact, he assumes at least implicit knowledge of the Trinity). What is significant is that Aquinas's overall position on these issues is typically both cautious and confident: cautious in stating an explicit cognitive content necessary for salvation, confident in stating the ubiquity of grace in moral choices.

Aquinas's restraint in describing the present states of non-Christians is instructive. It implies that Christian theology of religions should limit itself to a confident affirmation of the general possibility of salvation as something present or underway in the lives of non-Christians. But the endeavor to field an overly detailed account of how this can be the case for particular non-Christians who are Hindus, Buddhists, Muslims, or Jews inevitably risks underestimating the significance of the distinctive religious aims they intentionally pursue.

The endeavor to account for the salvation of non-Christians has taken the form primarily of allowing for the possibility of their possession of implicit faith. The impetus for this has come notably from an enormously influential scriptural text: "And without faith it is impossible to please God. For whoever would draw near to God must believe that he exists and that he rewards those who seek him" (Hebrews 11:6). This passage has generally been taken to mean that the disposition and exercise of supernaturally elevated faith are required for the salvation of all persons who have the capacity to reason. Properly speaking, such faith

10. Thomas Aquinas, *Summa theologiae*, 2a2ae, 7–8; *De veritate*, 14, 11; see *III Sent.* 25, 2, 1, ii.

responds to God not simply on the grounds of natural knowledge of him but on the grounds of the authority of God himself revealing. There has been disagreement in the tradition about the specific content to which this assent of faith is given. Historically there has been a consensus that the content of saving faith should extend certainly to knowledge of God's existence and his disposition to "reward those who seek him" and probably to belief in Christ and the Trinity as well. In the history of the discussion of these issues, several theories have been developed to account for what is regarded as an implication of these claims about the necessity of faith when they are considered in the light of the doctrine of the universal salvific will. It has been asserted that God provides the means by which every human being capable of reasoning can, before death, acquire the knowledge necessary to make an act of faith and love in him. The most influential of such theories are those that appeal to the possibility of implicit faith.

The traditional distinction between explicit and implicit faith has its primary use in illuminating aspects of the dispositions of Christians with respect to their adherence to and comprehension of central doctrines. "Implicit faith" designates in the first place the dispositions of one who is a member of the community, who accepts what is taught in it as true, right, and good, and who undertakes to pattern his life in accord with these teachings *even though* he may not be able fully to articulate all the teachings of his community in their totality and complexity. The disposition of faith of such a person can be said to be, to a certain extent, implicit.

A description of this sort draws attention to the theoretical possibility that what is accepted in a general way could be made explicit given sufficient further education and study. A definite content of valuations, beliefs, and practical doctrines exists and is assented to with varying degrees of comprehension. This content—though it is not fully exhibited—could be drawn out and explicated. A description of this sort also draws attention to the intellectual responsibility of an at least partial reliance on the knowledge and testimony of trustworthy authorities. What one member of the community accepts implicitly, others could and do articulate explicitly. As in other domains of knowledge and action, a religious person's reliance on the authority of competent individuals engaged in a community of discourse is both rational and appropriate.

Thus, according to standard teaching, the notion of implicit faith designates in part the unrealized capacity to exhibit in full the doctrines of the Christian community, and in part the reasonable disposition to accept on the word of trustworthy or official authorities what is the full account of the doctrines of this community. It should be noticed that the acceptance involved in the disposition of implicit faith extends not only to an intellectual assent to the truths of faith but also to the total commitment that characterizes the life of faith. Christian faith—implicit and explicit—concerns not only the adherence to certain beliefs but also the determination to give one's entire life a certain course according to the pattern fostered by the Christian community and sustained by its common life and worship.

The traditional distinction between explicit and implicit faith does not apply to the disposition of faith insofar as it can be said, on the model of interpersonal relations, to be the total response of the believer to God. The logic of the concept of faith is such as to exclude the notion of "having faith in someone who is not in some sense known." In ordinary discourse we speak of "implicit" faith or trust precisely when we wish to describe our dispositions with regard to persons whom we know. On the basis of previous experiences of their trustworthiness or reliability, we feel confident about their projected conduct on future occasions and we are even prepared to discount reports of uncharacteristic conduct in the past. Unless we have had real occasion to doubt them, we continue to have faith or trust in such persons. In such cases our faith is implicit in the sense that it does not require further confirmation but not in the sense that it could be made explicit—

though of course we could on certain occasions explain why it is reasonable or how we had just come to realize (and articulate explicitly) that we had always (implicitly) trusted or believed in someone. The use of the term "implicit" to describe our dispositions in such circumstances normally does not so much suggest a contrast with "explicit" dispositions. Rather, it designates the quality or degree of intensity in our faith. Conceivably, the expression "implicit faith" could in this sense be used to describe the nature of our confidence in God. But normally we speak simply of "faith" in order to describe this total or relational aspect of our religious dispositions as they are directed to God.

The application of the concept of "implicit faith" to the dispositions of persons who are not Christians represents an extension beyond the logical range of its normal use in theology. According to this extended usage, the notion does not designate one's general acceptance of teachings that one knows could be made more detailed and explicit and be nonetheless acceptable. Rather, in the case of the members of other religious communities, it designates the implicit acceptance of a revelation they explicitly reject or of which they are unaware. In this case what is unexpressed is the fundamentally right course that they have set for their lives (from the Christian point of view) and that could in principle be pointed out to them. Their explicit descriptions of their beliefs, dispositions, and conduct could with varying degrees of accuracy reflect their actual states of mind and being; but only a Christian description could be fully adequate. The intrinsic logical connection between "implicit" and "explicit" faith in Christians is loosened here to allow for the possibility of a partial or otherwise inadequately articulated adherence on the part of non-Christians to doctrines the knowledge of which is regarded as necessary for salvation as the Christianity community understands it.

The notion of implicit faith can be developed in combination with a variety of theories accounting for the possession of the requisite knowledge on the part of non-Christians and a variety of descriptions of the content of this knowledge. What is noteworthy about most versions of this extended usage of the notion is that they prescind from a condition that the standard theological use of the notion generally involves, that is, a potentially explicable and publicly identifiable body of teachings implicitly held (on the whole) on the authority of competent or official teachers. Versions of this extended usage that seek to incorporate the relational aspects of our dispositions and actions as they are directed to God in addition prescind from a condition of "implicit faith" in its ordinary use—explicit knowledge of the reliability of some existent in view of which confidence in its conduct in given circumstances is reasonable.

It may be that the traditional notion of implicit faith as applied to the dispositions of certain non-Christians would have a certain plausibility in circumstances of limited religious interaction. Such a theological formulation might be appropriate in circumstances where few if any non-Christians are actually encountered or where little is known about the doctrines of their communities. But in the present situation this notion inevitably suggests that the self-descriptions that the members of other religious communities might provide on the basis of their own doctrines could never give an adequate account of their dispositions. Nothing they could say in the course of proposing their doctrines would rule out the possibility that a theology of religions could define their states of mind and being in terms of implicit Christian faith. In view of the recommendation to engage in dialogue, a fullblown theory of implicit faith mounted to describe the dispositions of non-Christians seems incongruous.

Perhaps it would be best to avoid the concept of implicit faith in this context, unless some specific content in the beliefs of non-Christians can be identified as congruent with some specific content in Christian beliefs in particular instances, or at least to employ a more modest concept like "virtual faith." A theology of religions that incorporates the notion of prospective salvation can avoid the implausible descriptions of the present state of the members of other communities that are needed in order to ascribe salvific value to their present dispositions and conduct. The conceptual tools to do more are simply lacking.

About the most that could be said would be that a particular religious community may foster dispositions that advance its members partly along the way to fellowship with the Triune God. Aims can occur in ordered sequences, and priorities assigned to "higher" aims do not negate or exclude subordinate aims. It was observed in chapter 2 that a person could develop dispositions with a view to a certain aim without the awareness that the attainment of this aim afforded access to another. It might turn out that religious aims pursued as ultimate were themselves encompassed by an end yet more ultimate. Thus, Muslims or Buddhists could be said to develop dispositions conducive to the enjoyment of the true aim of life—fellowship with the Blessed Trinity—even though they do so in the light of conceptions that rule out personal relations either within God or in the ultimate state of enlightenment. The upshot would be that such persons could reach the threshold of the enjoyment of the true aim of life not only despite but also because of dispositions fostered in their communities, even though some of their doctrines are regarded as mistaken or incomplete from the Christian point of view.

Prospective Fellowship with God

But it is clear that this line of reflection veers perilously close to the very difficulties that this book has been concerned to avoid. The expressed finalities of Buddhist and Muslim patterns of life certainly do not envisage subordination to the finality commended by the Christian community. There is perhaps less danger of downplaying these distinctive finalities if judgments framed with this degree of detail were thought of as appropriate only in an eschatological perspective. This is the light in which to understand the attraction of what can be termed prospective accounts of the salvation of non-Christians, such as that proposed by George Lindbeck and others.[11] By projecting the moment of experienced salvation into the time of death or beyond death, Christian theology of religions in a prospective vein combines a confident affirmation of the possibility of salvation for non-Christians with respect for their distinctive doctrines about the true aim of life and for the finality of the dispositions they foster in their communities.

Recent prospective accounts of the salvation of non-Christians can be usefully amplified by appeal to the doctrine of purgatory. At first, it may strike the reader as foolhardy to invoke the doctrine of purgatory at this juncture—in effect, to try to resolve one set of difficulties with a proposal infinitely more problematic. Vexing problems beset the doctrine, notably: the nature of the intermediate state it assumes; the time, place, and imagery of purgatory; the range of intra-Christian disagreements about the doctrine. In fact, however, the doctrine has been well defended of late. If it is granted for the sake of discussion that the chief difficulties can be satisfactorily dealt with and resolved, then Christian theology of religions may be able to tap the potential of this neglected doctrine.

The doctrine of purgatory is formulated with a view to the enjoyment of the life to come by believers who die in the state of unrepented minor sin or with the lingering dispositional consequences of repented and forgiven patterns of sin. The doctrine envisages an intermediate state between death and the last judgment in which any personal obstacles (what Rahner calls a lack of integration) to the full enjoyment of the true end of life, fellowship with the Blessed Trinity, are eliminated. According to standard Catholic doctrine, purgatory does not provide an opportunity to reverse life-shaping decisions taken prior to death. This is the

11. Lindbeck, *The Nature of Doctrine*, 55–63, and "*Fides ex auditu* and the Salvation of Non-Christians," in *The Gospel and the Ambiguity of the Church*, ed. Vilmos Vajta (Philadelphia: Fortress Press, 1973), 91–123.

sense of saying that one's eternal fate is settled at death; individual judgment by Christ occurs immediately after death. Hence, the interval between individual judgment and the general judgment cannot be considered as one in which conversion could now occur when none had taken place prior to death, or that the fundamental orientation of one's life could be altered. The decisions taken in life cannot turn out to have been irrelevant to the shape of the life to come.

The point of the doctrine is that a certain kind of life may render one unfit for the *immediate* enjoyment of fellowship with the Blessed Trinity, even though one is ultimately destined for it. The dispositions to enjoy fellowship with the Blessed Trinity have not developed fully, though of course no contrary ("hellish") dispositions remain ineradicably entrenched. On this interpretation of the doctrine, it is not so much that God cannot abide imperfection as that in an unpurified state a human being could not fully enjoy God's company. An interval or experience of additional transformation—gained for us by Christ—is needed. It is not essential to the doctrine that purgatory be thought of as a place or duration, and certainly not a punishment by fire. What is crucial is that it allows for an interval (which may be thought of as instantaneous and coterminous with death) the essential feature of which is the experience of a necessary purification or transformation in view of the assured prospect of eternal bliss.

If this possibility is open to Christians, then surely there is no reason in principle to rule it out for non-Christians. According to Catholic doctrine, purgatory provides for an interval for the rectification of whatever is lacking in any human being who dies justified or in the state of grace, but unprepared for the full enjoyment of bliss.

The doctrine of purgatory permits Christian theology a wide measure of confidence about the salvation of non-Christians (just as much as it does for many imperfect Christians who are, for that matter, in the greater peril) without underestimating the distinctive aims they have pursued in life. Whatever transformation purgatory will entail for non-Christians, its purely cognitive side should not be exaggerated. The transformation of purgatory will not involve simply a disruptive "re-education" about the nature of the "transcendent," which—having been discovered to be radically other than one had supposed it to be—now demands a radical revision of one's beliefs. As we have noted, the pursuit of religious aims and the cultivation of religious dispositions not directly opposed to the enjoyment of fellowship with the Blessed Trinity can be viewed as in some sense preparatory for it. The doctrine of purgatory derives its force from convictions about the continuity between the earthly and the post-mortem life of those who die in the state of grace. Presumably, for non-Christians purgatory would involve the realization of the continuities as well as the discontinuities between what they had practiced and believed and what is indeed the case about the true aim of life.

But theology of religions strays beyond its limits here. Except that it must allow for this possibility and can broadly sketch its structure, theological analysis is not competent to specify in detail what this purifying interval will involve for individual human beings—rollicking religious imagination to the contrary notwithstanding. Proposals with an eschatological ring to them should be advanced in a judiciously restrained tone. The contribution that the doctrine of purgatory makes here is that it allows respect for the varieties of aims that religious people pursue in this life without ruling on the question of their bearing on the life to come.

Christian confidence about the salvation of non-Christians, when framed in terms of the notion of their prospective rather than hidden affiliation with the Christian community, is directly inspired and sustained by the specifically Christian account of God's plan for the world. According to the Christian story, this plan calls for the fidelity and testimony of a particular historical community. Eternal union with God constitutes the collective destiny of the human race. The Christian community bears witness to a set of divine promises, made first to the people of Israel, in which God himself undertakes to bring about this collective destiny. The Christian community moreover attests that these promises are now in principle fulfilled by the life, death, resurrection, and glory of Jesus Christ. In a way difficult to specify, the course of history is now permanently and irreversibly altered. God will not go back on his promises.

Although the Christian community's fidelity and testimony play a unique role in the ultimate fulfillment of the divine promises unsurpassably confirmed in Christ, it can never teach that these promises concern only itself. On the contrary, all the nations of the world have been made co-heirs of the divine promises. The Christian conviction about the universal significance of the agency of Christ in bringing this final consummation to term rests precisely on richly detailed narratives about the chosen people of Israel and the chosen One of God. If Christians can with confidence affirm the universality of salvation, then they can do so only on the grounds of their fidelity to their living Lord.

It by no means follows from the particular and unique role ascribed to Jesus Christ in central Christian doctrines that those who do not *now* acknowledge him will be permanently excluded from sharing in the salvation he both signifies and effects. Rather than attributing an implausible implicit faith in Christ to the members of other religious communities, theology of religions in a prospective vein contends that non-Christians will have the opportunity to acknowledge Christ in the future. This opportunity may come to them in the course of their lives here on earth or in the course of their entrance into the life to come. Certainly such a view accords well with specific doctrines about the nature and agency of Jesus Christ and with the distinctive doctrines of other communities.

In the Christian community, no theology of religions is likely to be regarded as fully consistent with central Christian doctrines if it does not permit a strong affirmation of the universality of salvation at least as a possibility. This doctrine rules assertions of the doctrines of grace and salvation in this way: no doctrines of grace and salvation can be genuinely Christian that in principle exclude any segment of humankind from the possibility of reaching its true and divinely promised destiny. The doctrine of the divine universal salvific will thus has a global or overall regulative force for the construal of central Christian doctrines and, by implication, of doctrines about other religions and their adherents. Overly detailed accounts of how this universal salvific will is exercised in the lives of individual non-Christians are likely to appear somewhat implausible and inappropriate in view of what such persons might be expected to say in the course of proposing their own doctrines and pursuing the aims commended by their communities.

A Christian theology of religions, having the broad contours outlined in this chapter, comprises a strong affirmation of the doctrine of the divine universal salvific will without prejudice to central Christian doctrines and without prejudice to the distinctive claims put forward by other communities. The Christian community will not regard itself "as the exclusive community of those who have a claim to salvation, but as the historically tangible vanguard" of a coming destiny it hopes to share with the whole human family.[12]

12. Karl Rahner, "Christianity and Non-Christian Religions," *Theological Investigations*, vol. 5, 133.

CHAPTER FOUR

Theology in Dialogue

THE nineteenth-century Japanese Buddhist scholar Enryo Inoue remarked once: "It is neither because I favor Sakyamuni [Gautama the Buddha] nor because I am prejudiced against Jesus that I uphold Buddhism and reject Christianity. It is simply because I love truth and hate untruth."[1] Similar statements could be culled from the writings of other scholars of Buddhist as well as non-Buddhist communities. This concern for truth exhibits itself particularly when one community seeks to define its own positions over against those of other communities. Inoue implies that his adherence to Buddhism represents, not an arbitrary allegiance, but a reflective conviction about the truth of Buddhist teachings.

At the same time, it is not unusual for a religious community to acknowledge that the truth about important matters can occur outside its own teachings. As K. Dhammananda remarked: "The Buddha stressed that no one religious teacher can reveal all the important manifestations of the truth for mankind. Most of the world's religious leaders have revealed certain aspects of the truth according to the circumstances that prevailed at that time. The Buddha explained that he had pointed out only the most important aspects of religion and the truth."[2] How it happens that truth

1. Quoted in Masao Abe, "Buddhism and Christianity as a Problem of Today," *Japanese Religion* 3 (1963), no. 2, 21.

2. Sri K. Dhammananda, *Why Religious Tolerance?* (Kuala Lumpur: Buddhist Missionary Society, 1974), 8.

can be found outside its authentic doctrines is the kind of issue addressed by a community's doctrines about other communities. Thus, without prejudice to the "historical uniqueness" of the Buddha's role in the "rediscovery" of the Dharma, Sangharakshita nonetheless insists that since "the Dharma states with a precision and clarity . . . those universal laws in accordance with which the attainment of Enlightenment by a human being takes place, and . . . the conditions upon which it depends and the means by which it must be achieved," knowledge about it is in principle accessible to any well-disposed inquirer.[3]

Among other things, these remarks express the conviction that Buddhist teachings have a universal relevance. These teachings are addressed to the widest possible audience and offer all human beings the opportunity to seek and attain the true aim of life. A further conviction is implied. The truth of Buddhist teachings can be supported at least in part by appeal to considerations drawn from commonly shared experiences of the world and of human existence within it. If Buddhist teachings possess a universal relevance, then it follows that they must interpret or at least speak to certain commonly recognizable features of human existence. Thus, in explanation of the wide acceptance that Buddhism and Christianity have enjoyed, the Buddhist scholar and philosopher Hajime Nakamura remarked that the beliefs and practices of these communities address "what may be described as universal problems, or questions raised and needs and aspirations expressed by men everywhere, irrespective of country, race or cultural differences; problems arising from our common experience of life itself with reference to man's condition, environment and destiny."[4]

The preceding chapters have sketched in broad strokes a Christian theology of religions that would be suited to current circum-

3. Sangharakshita, *A Survey of Buddhism*, 37.

4. Hajime Nakamura, *Buddhism in Comparative Light* (New Delhi: Islam and the Modern Age Society, 1975), 10–11.

stances of religious interaction. Many Christian communities approach these circumstances with a renewed esteem for other traditions and a readiness to engage in dialogue with their adherents. This seems to entail that the Christian theologian of religions should notice and take seriously the distinctive doctrines of other religious communities. When the soteriocentric principle is set aside, even if only experimentally, traditional Christian doctrines about other religions can be formulated in ways that acknowledge the varieties of aims pursued and commended by other communities. The Christian community's confidence in the availability of truth and salvation beyond its ambit can be expressed in terms of affirmations of the providential diversity of religions and of the prospective salvation of their adherents.

With this account of a theology *for* dialogue in place, we turn in this chapter to a consideration of theology *in* dialogue. This topic is, of course, as broad as Christian theology itself and as wide ranging as are the doctrines of our potential dialogue partners in Buddhist, Hindu, Muslim, and Judaic communities. The comments of the Buddhist scholars Inoue, Dhammananda, Sangharakshita, and Nakamura will help us to focus our discussion here on a topic of considerable significance for Christian theology in dialogue.

The remarks quoted above tell us something about how a religious community might go about securing its claim to the truth and rightness of its doctrines. In addition to resources afforded by its canon of scriptures and influential authors, a community is normally prepared to link its teachings with accepted or well-warranted knowledge about the world at large. There are variations from one community to the next about the extent to which their schemes of doctrines permit such connections. But the doctrinal schemes of the world's major religious communities generally do not seem to rule them out. Indeed, highly ramified doctrinal schemes normally comprise extensive interpretations of features of human existence and possess the capacity continually to incorporate new relevant knowledge. Such connections play an important role in interreligious dialogue and similar situations when a community needs to define its doctrines over against those of other communities. The presumption that their doctrinal schemes are not epistemically isolated allows the members of one community to propose and defend their teachings in ways that are cogent and understandable, even if not persuasive, to the members of other religious communities.

Like the Buddhist and other religious communities, the Christian community approaches dialogue with well-established convictions about the truth and rightness of its doctrines and about their bearing on the full range of human life, knowledge, and experience. We shall observe that, considered in this light, philosophical theology assumes a prominent role in Christian theology in dialogue.

A NEW CONVERSATION

In the Christian community, the whole meaning of human life can be expressed by saying that human beings are directed to union with God or, in more explicitly scriptural imagery, to the vision of God: we shall see him as he is (1 John 3:2). But the Christian belief that the true end of life is the beatific vision or union with God is affirmed today in a climate in which knowledge and appreciation of rival claims about the meaning and aim of human life may be expected to be widespread. According to sociologist Peter Berger's analysis, today's social and cultural climate is characterized by a wholesale and seemingly irreversible "pluralization of both institutions and plausibility structures," and thus by an immeasurable expansion of the realm of choice and decision in religious and other areas of life. Alternative views of the meaning of human life compete for attention with Christian beliefs in an enlarged marketplace of ethical and religious wisdom.[5] The teach-

5. Peter Berger, *The Heretical Imperative* (Garden City: Doubleday, 1979), 17.

ing functions of the Christian community at every level (catechetical, theological, and magisterial) are today inevitably exercised in dialogue with alternative positions, not the least important of which are those associated with the teachings of other religious communities.

As we have seen, different teachings about the focus of life as a whole appear to distinguish the overall patterns of life and belief that Christian, Buddhist, Hindu, Muslim, and Judaic communities foster in their members and commend to outsiders. With the increased religious interaction typical of our times has come a heightened awareness of these differences. In earlier chapters it was noted that genuine tolerance of other religious people presupposes an acknowledgment of the significance of these differences. It seems clear that the Christian community will need to take other communities' teachings into account as it engages in conversation with their members and as it develops its own doctrines about the focus of life as a whole.

The new conversation is different from another one that has preoccupied the Christian community in recent centuries. Modernity brought with it a pressing need for Christian communities to engage in dialogue with thinkers who built religious proposals into their philosophical positions. The intentions of some of these philosophers were friendly: they meant to offer support for Christian claims perceived to be under attack for one reason or another. Other philosophers were markedly unsympathetic to Christian claims. Increasingly the dialogue turned into a conversation with thinkers seeking to challenge central Christian claims about God, about revelation, about the course of history, about the reliability of the Bible, and the possibility of natural theology, about the meaningfulness of religious (that is, "Christian") discourse, and so on.

Such thinkers might adopt a religiously skeptical or atheistic point of view, or they might propose an independent religious philosophy, partially congruent and partially contrasting with the pattern of life and doctrines proposed by particular Christian communities. Very much at issue in these discussions were "religious" matters as these had come to be defined since the Enlightenment. It was during that period that the idea first seriously occurred to people on a large scale that one could be religious (by holding to some fundamental religious beliefs about God, human destiny, and the moral order) without being an adherent of any particular religious tradition (that is, without being Christian, Jewish, or Muslim). Furthermore, other thinkers seem to challenge the very scope of religious knowledge and explanation itself, which was seen to be in constant retreat before the inexorable advance of knowledge in the human and natural sciences. John Updike furnishes a graphic description of Christian theology's flight into ever-narrowing contexts of explanation: "In the sixteenth century astronomy, in the seventeenth microbiology, in the eighteenth geology and paleontology, in the nineteenth Darwin's biology all grotesquely extended the world-frame and sent churchmen scurrying for cover in ever smaller, shadowy nooks, little gloomy ambiguous caves in the psyche where even now neurology is cruelly harrying them, gouging them out of the multifolded brain like wood lice from under the lumber pile."[6]

This situation is in marked contrast to the one posed by religious interaction. Here, Christian communities confront, not merely personal religious philosophies, but massive and enduring bodies of religious wisdom and highly ramified systems of doctrines derived from sources as ancient and rich as any of their own. Furthermore, the challenges that arise from this encounter come not from religiously skeptical individuals but from religious communities advancing well-developed alternative conceptions of the ultimate aim of life and the pattern life ought to take in view of this aim.

Topics that fall under traditional natural or philosophical theology have a central, though perhaps unexpected, role to play in this new conversation. Arguments about the existence and nature

6. John Updike, *Roger's Version* (New York: Knopf, 1986), 32.

of the ultimate object of worship or quest in a religious community are fundamental to the overall strategy by which its particularlistic claim to universality is secured. This is true for the Christian no less than for other religious communities.

RELIGIOUS REFERENCES AND PREDICATIONS

To gain some perspective on this topic, imagine a conversation between a Muslim and a Buddhist about religious matters. After listening for a while, the Buddhist asks the Muslim to identify the term "Allah," which has come up several times in the conversation. The Muslim replies that Allah is the one who spoke to Muhammad, as recounted in the Qu'ran. Although the Buddhist is not yet familiar with the Qu'ran and knows little about Muhammad, he begins to catch the drift. He asks whether Allah is like one of the gods of the Hindu pantheon who appear occasionally to human beings. No, replies the Muslim: Allah is God, the only one God, who rewards the just and punishes the wicked, and who can never be seen by human eyes. The Buddhist continues to be puzzled. So the Muslim invites him to observe the beauty and orderliness of the natural world. Allah is the one who made and preserves all this. The whole meaning of life is to live in submission to him ("Islam"). And so the conversation might proceed.

Suppose that during the course of the conversation the Buddhist should refer to "Nirvana." Since the Buddhist seems to attach such great importance to the reality designated by this term, the Muslim begins to assume that the Buddhist might be talking about God. Is Nirvana a name for God? No, Nirvana is not any kind of God. Indeed, it is not a presently existing entity at all. It is a state of being. The Muslim needs help in grasping this. So the Buddhist might now invite him to think of intense experiences he has had that have been so absorbing that he has felt transported outside of himself. Nirvana is something like this, only ineffably more so. The chief aim of life is to attain this blissful state by following the Excellent Eightfold Path.

In each of these cases, some fact or state of affairs within experience serves as a starting point for a reference to the focus of life in the Muslim and Buddhist communities respectively. The Muslim points to the observable pattern of things and attributes this to the agency of Allah. The Buddhist invokes a certain range of intense states of experience in order to identify Nirvana.

This hypothetical conversation throws light on a certain group of arguments that seem to be logically required if a religious community is to support its claims about the focus of life as a whole.[7] Referential arguments of this kind function logically to introduce a logical subject—the focus of life—into the discourse of a religious community. The style of such arguments varies widely with the range of distinctive beliefs about the focus of life among religions. What are usually called "arguments for the existence of God" in the Christian and other theistic communities thus have formal parallels in nontheistic doctrinal schemes.

A word about the logic of references in general discourse will throw light on special problems posed for religious references. When I speak about the "tulips in the cloister garden," an ostensive reference is enough for you to know what I am talking about: all I have to do is point to them. If I say that I have vacationed on Barbados, however, simple ostension won't do: you will need an atlas if you are unfamiliar with the island and its location. If I start speaking about protons and neutrons, ostension will fail completely: something more is needed to establish a reference for subatomic or theoretical particles. In order to get along in most conversations about particular subjects, of course, we rely on broad general knowledge for supplying the required references. It is rare that something utterly unheard of and unfamiliar comes up for discussion.

Religious references are more complex. In most religious com-

7. This account of arguments in religious discourse is dependent upon William A. Christian, Sr., *Meaning and Truth in Religion* (Princeton: Princeton University Press, 1964), 185–237.

munities, even those with relatively undeveloped doctrinal schemes, the focus of life and worship is normally not thought to be identical with any sense-perceptible object within ordinary experience. We saw above that talk about "Allah" and "Nirvana" requires starting points in experience, which orient us in the right "direction" to see what is being referred to. But it turns out that more extended arguments will be needed to bridge the gap between ordinary experience and the focal objects and/or states at the center of religious affirmations.

Let's proceed directly to the contexts defined by theistic religious affirmations as in the Christian community. Two modes of reference play a central role in referential arguments for religious doctrines whose focus is a transcendent agent. These are references that construe certain observable facts or patterns in experience as (1) regular or (2) extraordinary effects caused by the transcendent agent.

The first type of reference appeals to regular or persistent features of the natural order like perishability, or design, or finality, and so on. Arguments are framed to show that the whole natural order exhibiting such features is brought into and preserved in existence by the transcendent agent. Jewish, Muslim, and Christian theologians have developed many versions of such arguments, usually in connection with some metaphysical schemes, employing broadly Platonic or Aristotelian conceptualities, or hybrids of these. The second type of reference appeals to extraordinary or unusual facts or events—whether straightforwardly miraculous or simply nonregular. Normally such events have been recounted in the sacred literature of the community or the testimony of its leaders and saints.

As a kind of shorthand, we can say that these two types of reference are distinguished by their appeal to nature on the one hand, or to history on the other. References and arguments of the first type have a broader sweep, logically speaking, than those of the second type, for two reasons. First, particular events with a religious import belong to the larger class of historical events and are thus subject to the principles of observation and explanation applicable to events generally. Secondly, the extraordinary events that function as the starting point for religious references are reported in confessional narratives and are in principle subject to nonconfessional explanations.

A third type of reference should be mentioned here. It takes as its starting point certain features of the subjective states of human beings. Insofar as some of these states have the character of regular or extraordinary effects caused by a transcendent agent, this mode of reference is not clearly distinct from the first two. But their designation as a third type is justified by the logical peculiarity they exhibit: references of this type are largely self-certifying. They depend for their force, not on observation and publicly shared experiences, but on testimony about private or interior experiences of God, or on necessary entailments of concepts about God, or on recognition of the pervasive law-abidingness of human beings, or on the widespread conviction of many people that there is a God, and so on.

Another group of arguments can be identified in the hypothetical conversation we have been considering. These are arguments that serve to keep the discourse moving, once a successful reference has gotten the conversation off to a good start. When the participants have some idea of the objects or states of existence to which terms like "Allah" and "Nirvana" refer, then the way is open for descriptions of them. Thus, the Muslims will go on to assert that Allah is holy, and the Buddhist that Nirvana is the fullness of bliss and the absence of bliss. To advance and develop these kinds of assertions, arguments in support of predications would be needed. How can these and other attributes be ascribed to entities or states that transcend sense perception? Do such predications have properly assertive or only evocative force? Why are some primary ranking predicates appropriate and others excluded? Arguments in support of a religious community's descriptions of that upon which its pattern of life is focused would be needed to address these and related questions. In the Christian community, talk about the divine attributes falls into this category of argument.

In one respect, the hypothetical conversation sketched above is misleading, in that it suggests that such arguments have mainly apologetical uses in discussions between the members of a religious community and nonmembers. In fact, however, the primary logical setting of both referential and predicational religious arguments is internal to the religious scheme itself. Such arguments serve to locate the central affirmations of a religious community with reference to the widest possible conceptual map. In effect, they show that a doctrinal scheme has redrawn the map of human existence in the world. Highly ramified doctrinal schemes are field-comprehensive—to switch metaphors—and, although they do not generate everything, they do normally interpret and encompass wide ranges of knowledge and experience. The doctrinal schemes of the world's major religious communities seem to be field-comprehensive in this sense.

Referential and predicational arguments function chiefly to signal and explicate this field-comprehensiveness of a community's doctrines, their universal scope and relevance. Although important, their apologetical or dialogical uses are subsidiary to their internal uses. Arguments of these types serve complex purposes in understanding the whole of a doctrinal scheme, since they show how a community's doctrines connect with all sorts of human concerns, experiences, and knowledge.

These two forms of arguments—referential arguments and arguments to support predications—are familiarly known in the Christian community under the tags "natural theology" or "philosophical theology." But these forms of arguments are not peculiar to the Christian scheme. As the hypothetical conversation above suggests, Christian forms of these arguments seem to have analogues or parallels in other communities as well. Such arguments seem to be required by the logical structure of the discourse of religious communities: they help to secure the particularistic claims to universality that all communities appear to make for their doctrines.

It is hard to see how the new interreligious conversation could keep up its momentum if the participating religious communities were unwilling to mount any referential and predicational arguments in support of their doctrines. This is an important lesson for Christian theology in dialogue. It is also a refreshing one. After having undergone relentless critique in the course of the Christian community's conversation with modern philosophers since the Enlightenment, Christian forms of these arguments turn out to have an extended viability in Christianity's new and more challenging conversations with Buddhist, Hindu, Muslim, and Judaic communities in the present day.

PHILOSOPHICAL THEOLOGY IN HISTORICAL PERSPECTIVE

Generally speaking, debate between the Christian community and its philosophical critics has centered on the validity of referential patterns of argument. There is no possibility here of charting in detail the complex history of this debate, except insofar as it bears on the prospects for continued use of these forms of arguments in the new interreligious conversation now gathering momentum.

We have seen that referential arguments normally involve appeals of three types: to the natural course of things in the world (e.g., the design of the universe), to particular events in history (e.g., miracles), or to subjective states or experiences (e.g., the human sense of ultimacy). In classical Christian theology, references of all three types, whether well developed or implicit, were interwoven and mutually reinforcing. Arguments of the first type played an increasingly prominent role in the medieval period, with the growth of interest in and knowledge about the physical world. But with the coming of modernity, arguments of the first type were subjected to a devastating critique from which they have never fully recovered. In the wake of this critique, arguments of the second and third types—appealing to history and the self—have gradually taken over the field.

This development has posed considerable difficulties for Christian theology as it strives to secure the universal scope and relevance of the Christian confession. For it has long been recognized that logical rigor and objectivity decrease as one moves from the first to the third type of referential argument. While appeals to subjective experiences and states possess a great psychological interest and intensity, they are largely self-certifying. Appeals to history rest on the reliability of confessional documents or on speculative philosophies of history. Without the reinforcement of arguments of the first type, referential arguments warranted exclusively by historical or subjective data are peculiarly vulnerable logically speaking. A few remarks about the history of modern theology will serve to confirm this judgment.

Two developments in particular had decisive consequences for the internal or doctrinal uses of arguments of the first type. In the first place, the connection of these arguments with the doctrinal schemes of Christian and other theistic communities was severed. This separation developed on two fronts. First, with the Enlightenment such arguments were pried from their doctrinal settings in order to specify the kernel of natural religion within (and eventually opposed to) revealed or positive religion. In effect such arguments were turned against the doctrinal schemes they were developed to support. Secondly, their apologetic virtualities were increasingly exploited: they served to demonstrate to skeptical outsiders the "reasonableness" of Christianity. As a result, such arguments came to be viewed as establishing part of the subject matter of distinct fields of inquiry—"natural theology" or "philosophical theology"—largely independent of the doctrinal contexts of particular theistic traditions.

A second development had a more serious and wide-ranging impact on the viability of the first type of reference. This came with Immanuel Kant's critique of what he took to be all versions of such arguments. The widespread acceptance of this critique set the stage for the historical and subjective turns executed in much nineteenth-century Protestant and twentieth-century Catholic theology.

Kant (1724–1804) contended that such arguments fail to deliver the results they promise. They suppose the possibility of moving from metaphysical assertions about the structures of things in themselves conceived as a single effect to God as the First Cause. In fact, such cosmological and teleological arguments (as Kant tagged them) are covertly versions of the ontological argument. Tied to the rationalist conception of metaphysics in which he was reared, Kant contended that such arguments traffic in concepts (causality, contingency, design, being, world, God) that derive not from experience but from the mental apparatus used to structure incoming perceptions. Such arguments achieve no more than the ontological argument: they unpack the content of the concept of God rather than showing that he exists.[8]

Kant's combined critique of metaphysics and classical natural theology was understood by many philosophers and theologians to have permanently undermined the plausibility of arguments of the first type. Insofar as theologians accepted this critique as definitive, they turned to arguments of the second and third types to support Christian affirmation. G. W. F. Hegel (1770–1831) in effect transformed the whole of the philosophy of history into an all-encompassing dialectical argument of the second type. Friedrich Schleiermacher (1768–1834) welcomed the Kantian critique of metaphysics and natural theology as a liberation of theology from metaphysical categories. He substituted appeal to the God-relation given in the very structure of the self for appeal to nature or history. Subsequently, even when they did not adopt the details

8. Immanuel Kant, *Critique of Pure Reason*, trans. Norman Kemp Smith (New York: Macmillan, 1929), I, Second Division, chap. 3, sections 3–7 (495–531).

of Hegel's or Schleiermacher's programs, theologians were deeply influenced by the turns to history and the self that these programs commended. This influence was felt differently in Reformation, Orthodox, and Roman Catholic communities.

In large measure, the subsequent history of theology in Reformation communities has seen the erosion of theological positions that took these turns. Without the massive reinforcement provided by the Hegelian system, the appeal to history has proved to be extraordinarily vulnerable as a support for theological affirmation in the face of the combined challenge of Feuerbach, Marx, Freud, Darwin, and the historical-critical study of the Bible. Despite its continued appeal, the turn to the structures of self-consciousness is widely regarded as having received a deathblow from Ludwig Feuerbach (1804–72) and (somewhat derivately) Karl Marx (1818–83) and Sigmund Freud (1856–1939). Feuerbach's critique of Christian affirmation seems an inevitable response to the retreat of theologians from the field of natural theology classically conceived as an enterprise involving appeal to some accounts of a nonsubjective order. A "natural theology" rooted exclusively in some account of the transcendent dynamism or structure of human subjectivity relies on self-certifying propositions about internal experiences. Feuerbach can be construed as having fixed on this weakness in contending that theological concepts of God objectify human traits, aspirations, ideals, and perfections and project them onto a transcendent realm. The profoundly influential polemic against natural theology associated with the theology of Karl Barth (1886–1968) may be construed as an acknowledgment of the force of Feuerbach's critique of the subjective turn. Barth secures the divine identity, as essentially independent of the human reality, by basing it radically in the divine act of revelation and the narrative it engenders. Theology either begins with this revelation and its overarching narrative or falls prey to human hypostatizations masquerading as God.

The move toward postmodern positions among American Protestant theologians received a powerful stimulus from Barth's reading of the history of nineteenth-century theology. Acceptance of the Kantian critique of referential arguments of the first type and acknowledgment of the failure of arguments of the second and third types has done much to shape theology in contemporary Reformation communities. Theologians who have been influenced by Barth are forging an ingenious combination of resolutely anti-Cartesian Anglo-American analytical philosophy and continental hermeneutics, to fill the role of discredited referential arguments. Postliberal theologians can be distinguished from revisionists not with respect to background assumptions about these matters (which they largely share) but with respect to the role in theological affirmation they accord to specifically Christian language and narrative.

The response to modernity has been somewhat delayed in the theology of the Roman Catholic and Orthodox communities. This is especially clear in Roman Catholic theology, in which the more markedly defensive reaction of the nineteenth century gradually gave way to the welcoming response of the forty or so years spanning the pre- and post-conciliar periods in this century. The short-lived (at least among Catholic theologians) neo-scholastic revival is perceived by many to have provided only a temporary bulwark against the tides of modernity pressing against it. As might be expected, Catholic strategies for dealing with modernity's challenge to classical natural theology have matched earlier Protestant moves. The twentieth-century transcendental turn in Catholic theology, associated especially with the work of Karl Rahner, roughly parallels the nineteenth-century turn to the subject in Protestant theology. The prevailing Rahnerian (if not Rahner's) theology in the Catholic community exhibits remarkable formal and material similarities to modern Protestant theological positions. But transcendental styles are giving way to aesthetic, critical, and hermeneutical styles as Catholic theology yields to the pressures of anti-Cartesian developments in Protestant theology and in contemporary philosophy.

The ongoing conversation between Christian theology and

modern western philosophy has not favored referential arguments of any of the traditional types. In effect, nature, history, and the self have yielded to language and narrative as the context for theological affirmation. In the perspective of the history of theology in the Christian community and of the new conversation with the other religious communities, this context seems a sharply narrowed one.

The encounter with other religious communities invites Christian theology to develop its agenda with a view to the internal requirements of Christian discourse as a form of discourse exhibiting certain structural features—among them a fairly straightforward claim to the existential force (in the logical sense) and truth of primary doctrines that convey beliefs. Certain patterns of argument arise in response to this logical requirement for forms of reasoning that will secure the community's particularistic claim to universality for its doctrines. Philosophical theology in the Christian and other theistic traditions, and its cognates in nontheistic religions, comprise important sets of arguments developed to support claims of this sort. It is not clear that a religious community could maintain such a claim if it refrained from developing any arguments for it. It has been an unfortunate outcome of the conversation with skeptical modern philosophers that Christian confidence in the possibility and importance of such arguments has been gradually undermined.

One of the more challenging tasks for Christian theology in dialogue is to recover the broadest possible context in which to secure the fundamental claims of the Christian community. It can be expected that the claims of other communities will be advanced in the same logical space. As we have seen, claims to a universal relevance are typical of the doctrinal schemes of the world's major religious communities. Respect for other communities and recognition of the distinctiveness of their doctrines provide some of the impetus for developments of new forms of referential and predicational arguments for primary Christian doctrines.

Traditional theology furnishes perhaps unexpected resources for postmodern Christian theology as it seeks to develop arguments of this sort. The work of Thomas Aquinas can be of some help here. For one thing, Aquinas is innocent of the key moves that have been the subject of such vigorous attack in postmodern philosophy and theology: the quest for a unitary method for all knowledge and inquiry ("foundationalism"), the conflation of epistemology with metaphysics, and the separation of consciousness from bodiliness. Furthermore, Aquinas's theology furnishes a rich resource for exhibiting the logic of referential and predicational patterns of argument, as they function both in the Christian scheme itself and in interreligious dialogue.

Naturally it is neither possible nor desirable to repristinate Aquinas as if the intervening centuries had evaporated. As Bernard Williams recently remarked in another context: "There is certainly more to be said for . . . [traditional understandings of ethics] than much progressive thought has allowed; indeed there is more to be said for them than there is for much progressive thought. But even if one grants value to traditional knowledge, to try to suppress reflection in that interest can only lead to disaster, rather as someone who finds that having children has disrupted her life cannot regain her earlier state by killing them."[9] Christian philosophical theology has been permanently transformed by the past two centuries of debate. Nonetheless, as will become clear, Aquinas's treatment of these issues retains much of its cogency when considered in the light of the new interreligious conversation.

In addition to aiding our understanding of the logic of references and predications, study of Aquinas helps to expose certain deficiencies in some current accounts of these patterns of argu-

9. Bernard Williams, *Ethics and the Limits of Philosophy* (Cambridge: Harvard University Press, 1985), 168. On the absence of "Cartesianism" in Aquinas, see, for example, Anthony Kenny, *Aquinas* (New York: Hill and Wang, 1979), 27–31.

ment as they bear on interreligious conversations. We shall observe, to put it briefly, that in their current influential versions, inclusivists say too much and pluralists say too little: inclusivists tend to exaggerate the probative force of Christian references, while pluralists seem to attenuate the potential range of religious predications. In these ways, prominent pluralist and inclusivist positions tend to minimize the significance of religious differences. Christian theology in dialogue needs an account of Christian references and predications that reflects the seriousness of these differences and hence the import of the interreligious conversation whose challenge it embraces.

REFERRING TO THE TRIUNE GOD

Monastic communities from the Buddhist and Christian traditions have been in the forefront of the newly blossoming conversation among the world's major religions. Recently, a delegation of Buddhist bhikkhus and bhikkhunis (monks and nuns) visited several Christian monasteries across the United States. Imagine what such a visit would be like, say in a monastic community of contemplative Dominican nuns.

As they followed the daily monastic routine, the Buddhist visitors would find many practices and attitudes familiar to them from their own communities. Despite the striking contrast of their saffron robes with the black and white of the Dominicans, they would see in the common garb of the nuns the same singleness of religious purpose and commitment to simplicity of life that they have learned from the Buddha. The silence, the discipline, the early rising, the unpretentious fare, the manual labor, the chanting of prayer, the care and attention bestowed on the small details of life, indeed the sheer regularity of the daily schedule—all would make the Buddhist travelers feel at home.

A sufficiently leisurely visit would surely provide opportunities for conversation about their respective forms of life. Perhaps such conversation between the Buddhist visitors and their Dominican hosts would disclose similarities in the very rationale for their characteristic practices and comportment. The nuns would tell some of their favorite stories, particularly the one about how St. Dominic founded a community of nuns before ever getting around to organizing the friars. In addition, given the large measure of daily public prayer and liturgy in the Dominican monastic schedule, conversation would undoubtedly turn to the style and content of these activities.

At this point, the Dominican hosts would surely have to mention God. For they would not get too far along in discussing their worship without mentioning the one who is invoked continually in its psalms, antiphons, hymns, and prayers. Indeed, they might report to their Buddhist visitors, God is at the very center of the Dominican contemplative life. From their worship and love of God radiates the inner meaning of all the activities of their daily life. They are supposed to live, as the Dominican rule expresses it, "free for God alone." The God whom we love, they would say, has loved us first. He is the God of Abraham, Isaac, and Jacob, the God who saved us in Christ and who abides with us in his Spirit. Moreover, he is the God who inspired and sustained St. Dominic, the selfsame God to whom Dominican nuns like Catherine de Ricci, Margaret of Hungary, and countless others have been praying throughout the ages, the God who is present to us now even as we speak. And so the conversation would proceed.

A conversation about God among a group of Buddhist and Dominican monastic people would presumably make for some fairly stimulating talk indeed. But we must take our leave of it for the time being. For our purposes, the point of imagining this hypothetical encounter is that it helps us to see that Christian references to God in such a setting would take, at least initially, a markedly scheme-specific form. To express this point somewhat technically, we could say that the Triune God would appear as the principal character in an overarching narrative, as it were, which stretches over the whole length and breadth of his engagement with humankind, and extends to embrace present and future experience and events. References to him normally would take the form of narrations of his activities as reported in the Scriptures, celebrated in the round of the liturgical hours, days, and seasons, recounted in the lives of holy people, and so on.

Implicit in these scheme- or narrative-specific references is a broader one. The Triune God who is worshiped in the Christian community is none other than the cause of the world. Some expressions of this conviction would eventually emerge in some form during the course of the hypothetical conversation between Buddhists and Christians described above. To the question, Who is it that you worship in your prayer? the Christian would first respond, the God of Abraham, Isaac, and Jacob, the God made known to us in Christ. To the further question, But who is *he*? an apt Christian response would be, the God whom we worship is the cause of the world. Still, the conviction itself does not depend for its logical force on occasions of interreligious (or apologetic) conversations when it might come to be expressed explicitly. Christian confession and worship of God imply the belief that the scope of divine activity and engagement is as wide as the universe itself, and wider. Indeed, the God who is worshiped is, absolutely speaking, unlimited in his range of interest and power.

These considerations help to illumine the theological role of arguments for the existence of God. Their presence in early pages of Aquinas's *Summa theologiae* does not signal a methodological doubt such that Christian theology cannot go about its business until it has "proven" the existence of its subject.[10] This possibility is ruled out from the start by Aquinas's prior description of the nature of theological inquiry. To assert that theology gets its subject matter from revelation implies that faith in God constitutes one of the principles of the inquiry. The Triune God is already "in place," so to speak, in his full, scheme-specific characterization. The one confessed as Father, Son, and Holy Spirit is the

10. Thomas Aquinas, *Summa theologiae*, 1a. 2, 1–2.

cause of the world. Referential patterns of argument in theology serve not so much to establish God's existence as to secure the particularistic claim to universality that the Christian community makes for its doctrines.

Arguments for the existence of God function to secure this universal claim. Beginning with observable or generalized features of the world like causality, finality, and design, such arguments affirm the divine agency as the source of such features and of the world order as a whole. Whatever their logical merits or probative force, their position at the beginning of the theological inquiry (according to Aquinas's procedure) signals the logical space that Christian claims are understood to occupy. The arguments for the existence of God in the second question of Aquinas's *Summa theologiae* (the celebrated "Five Ways") thus function to locate Christian worship, nurture, practice, and belief on the widest possible conceptual map. The Triune God who is adored, proclaimed, and confessed in the Christian community has not only a local, narrative, or contextual reference within the usage of a particular cultural and linguistic community; even more, he is none other than the cause of the world.

Since such arguments are developed in connection with scientific and metaphysical claims, it has sometimes been objected that they mark the intrusion of alien conceptual categories and claims into a properly theological (and hence scripturally based) inquiry. But, according to the construal of Aquinas being suggested here, such a complaint misses the mark. These arguments do not displace but rather presuppose the reading of Scripture as a "canonically and narrationally unified and internally glossed . . . whole centered on Jesus Christ, and telling the story of the dealings of the Triune God with his people and his world in ways that are typologically . . . applicable to the present."[11] In effect, Aquinas

11. George A. Lindbeck, "Scripture, Consensus and Community," in *Biblical Interpretation in Crisis*, ed. Richard John Neuhaus (Grand Rapids: Eerdmans, 1989), 75.

can be construed as addressing the question (here and in subsequent discussions of the divine nature and agency, of angelic and human natures, and, finally and decisively, of Jesus Christ as divine-human agent): what must be true of the main characters of the Christian narrative for it to have the features Christians claim for it, truth and "followability"? Natural science, metaphysics, psychology, and other "secular" inquiries contribute as needed or well suited to filling out these complex characterizations. A literary analogy may help at this juncture. In a critical study of Melville's *Moby Dick*, for example, the complex narrative need not be continually retold in the course of literary analysis of the motivations and structure of the main characters. In somewhat the same way, in the *Summa theologiae* Aquinas presumes his readership's detailed familiarity with the Christian narrative in order to show or, more correctly, to remove obstacles to seeing that its central claims are true and its chief injunctions are followable.

The initial referential arguments are harnessed to this larger theological purpose. They serve primarily internal theological purposes in sustaining the broadest possible context for Christian affirmation, in connection not only with the doctrine of God but also with the doctrines of grace, christology, sacraments, and so on throughout the Christian scheme. They serve subsequently as the warrant or legitimation (logically speaking) for locating such affirmations, case by case, with reference to a variety of objective states of affairs.

Precisely because of their logical function in securing the universal scope of Christian claims, such arguments naturally come to serve purposes beyond the internal ones. Thus, because they press the truth and rightness of Christian claims by appealing to commonly shared experiences and knowledge, they may have a role in persuading outsiders to adopt the Christian pattern of life. But of more immediate concern here is the function of such arguments in the setting of interreligious conversations, where the claims of other communities are advanced in the same logical space.

Thus, for example, some version of arguments for the existence of God would be needed in conversations between Buddhists and Christians. Segments of the Buddhist community seem to be nontheistic in their doctrines, and their canonical and commentatorial literatures possess highly subtle explanations for the prevalence of the theistic beliefs in other religious traditions. Presumably, in conversation with members of such Buddhist communities, Christians would need to invoke patterns of referential argument analogous to those sketched by Aquinas in the Five Ways. A readiness to advance such arguments would be a way of taking Buddhist objections to theistic beliefs seriously. The notion of causation that is intrinsic to these arguments would presumably offer wide scope for debate. Theories of causation play a crucial role in the Buddhist account of the conditions of human existence that need to be transcended if the round of rebirths is to be escaped and Nirvana attained. In addition, given the markedly empirical orientation of Buddhist patterns of reflection and argument, there is considerable scope here for empirically based discussions such as those merely adumbrated in the Five Ways and similar arguments. Current scientific knowledge of the origins and structure of the universe would presumably be admitted as relevant by both Christian and Buddhist participants in such a conversation. Hence, the Five Ways could not be invoked without appropriate revisions reflecting the considerable advances in scientific knowledge of the relevant issues since Aquinas's time.

It is clear, then, that referential patterns of argument of the first type, appealing to objective states of affairs in the world, would have an important place in interreligious conversations. This kind of argument presupposes a field broad enough to sustain such conversations. The issues would be joined in a common logical field, so to speak, where rival particularistic claims to universality are taken seriously and debated. The participants' readiness to advance such arguments would make it possible for a true meeting of minds, though not necessarily agreement, to occur.

Naturally, other starting points for references would have their place in such conversations. But it seems clear that, in order to rise to the occasion (logically speaking), appeals to history, narratives, texts, personal experiences, and the like would need to be combined with referential arguments having features of the natural order of things as their starting point.

We need to consider at this juncture an influential inclusivist version of a referential argument that appeals, not to regular features of the world, but to the structure of human knowledge of the world. In his philosophical theology, Karl Rahner developed a referential argument in connection with his analysis of the conditions for the possibility of human knowledge of God's existence and, in addition, for the possibility of human recognition of a divine revelation. In its original setting the argument was not developed for service in theology of religions. But given the theory of religion it implied, the argument had important ramifications for Rahner's broadly inclusivist construal of traditional Christian doctrines about other religions.[12]

According to this argument, the capacities to exercise concepts and beliefs and to desire actual or possible existents presuppose the possession and exercise of the concept of being. But the concept of being, because it always eludes full conceptualization, points beyond itself to Absolute Being. Further, since Absolute Being is Absolute Mystery—or that which unconditionally engages human beings—and Absolute Mystery is identified in the primary doctrines of the Christian community as the Triune God, then it follows that every exercise of intellectual and affective capacities necessarily engages human beings with the Triune God. Thus, the Christian reference to God is secured by means of a transcendental argument showing that God is none other than

12. Karl Rahner presents an extended argument in philosophical theology in his works *Spirit in the World*, trans. William Dych (New York: Herder & Herder, 1968), especially 132–236, and *Hörer des Wortes*, ed. J. B. Metz (Munich: Kosel-Verlag, 1963).

that entity beyond all entities, who unconditionally engages human beings in all knowing and willing.

In Rahner's theology of religions, the Christian community's particularistic claim to universality and an ascription of a salvific value to other religions are supported by a further argument that develops certain consequences of the transcendental argument sketched above. It follows from the main argument that all religious experience, expression, and conduct have for their object the Absolute Mystery who is identified in Christian doctrines with the Triune God. This complex argument combines premises from the philosophy of mind, metaphysics, and the philosophy of religion in order to extend the Christian doctrine of uncreated grace (construed in terms of Rahner's concept of divine self-communication) to an account of the presence and quasi-sacramental operations of grace in non-Christian religions. According to this account the doctrines and patterns of life of other religions—as externalizations of a supernaturally elevated experience of a universally accessible divine self-communication in grace—can be viewed as affording their adherents a real contact with the Triune God on whom the Christian pattern of life is centered. Hence it is possible to develop in a single overall argument both an assertion of the universal relevance of Christian doctrines and an ascription of salvific value to their doctrines, institutions, and other forms of religious expression.

The basic valuation of a religious community's scheme of doctrines ascribes to the object (e.g., the Triune God) or state of being (e.g., Nirvana) on which its pattern of life is centered some unrestricted primacy-ranking predicates (e.g., most holy, perfect in being, supreme goal of life). Thus the basic valuation of the Christian scheme can be conveyed in a statement like this: the Blessed Trinity is most holy. The basic valuation of Buddhism can be expressed in this way among others: Nirvana is the supreme goal of life.

A general theory of religion would, among other things, strive to give an account of basic valuations in religious communities by developing some broadly applicable value for the predicate terms in doctrines that propose basic valuations. Since there is a great variety of possible predicates in the characteristic discourse of particular religious communities and in the religious domain generally, a general theory of religion would be expected to propose some value for as many such predicates as could be adduced.

Basic valuations are different from general theories in a notable way. Religious doctrines that convey basic valuations always assign values *both* to the subjects and to the predicates in expressions of the form "*m* is *P*," where *m* stands for that existent or state of being on which a religious community's pattern of life is centered and *P* stands for predicates ascribed to *m*. But general theories of religion propose values only for predicates. A theory of religion would fail to be a general theory if it assigned some value to *m* in such expressions. It would be more like a religious doctrine that conveyed a basic valuation to which alternative valuations could be proposed, rather than like a general theory that sought to explain something of the diversity of basic religious valuations among existing religious communities.

Rahner's argument, as outlined above, appeals in part to what appears to be a general theory of religion. If we rephrase the term "Absolute Mystery" as it is used in Rahner's theology of religions, we will have an expression that could serve as a value for *P* in a general theory of religion. Thus, let us say that "Absolute Mystery" is equivalent to "that which ought unconditionally to engage human beings."

Employing this predicate value in a general theory of religion, we could say that it would be a sign that some utterance in the discourse of a particular religious community expressed its basic valuation if the phrase "that which ought unconditionally to engage human beings" could plausibly be substituted for predicate terms like "holy" or "perfect in being," and so on, which appeared in this utterance. Thus, in terms of such a general theory of religion, it would be possible to restate the basic valuations of the Christian and Buddhist communities in the following ways:

the Triune God is that which ought unconditionally to engage human beings; Nirvana is that which ought unconditionally to engage human beings. Thus, a general theory of religion would help persons engaged in religious inquiries or arguments to formulate common terms by means of which basic religious valuations could be compared and contrasted, or simply studied as samples of the rich variety of discourse in the religious domain.

But we can notice a difficulty in the way the predicate value "that which ought unconditionally to engage human beings" is employed in the argument laid out above. Although this predicate value appears to be used as the basis for a general theory of religion, the argument itself seems not to envisage (logically speaking) the application of this predicate value to the referents of any basic valuations other than the Christian one. Although it would be possible to employ this predicate value in a general theory of religion (in saying: predicates in basic religious valuations assert of some referent that it is the object or state of being that ought unconditionally to engage human beings), in the argument above it would be used (as "Absolute Mystery" is in fact used) to define the referent of the Christian basic valuation. According to this argument the existent with which all human beings are unconditionally engaged in all religious communities is the Triune God. There are in effect no self-consistent alternative basic religious valuations; there are only more or less inadequate versions of the single basic version which is given fullest expression in the Christian scheme and pattern of life.

We are now in a better position to grasp the difficulty posed by this inclusivist version of a referential argument in the setting of interreligious conversations: by importing a basic religious valuation into an apparently general theory of religion (developed in the context of philosophy of religion), the argument presupposes what it must in fact show. It sets out to show that the Christian community expresses more adequately what is partially embodied in other religions. But instead of showing this it presupposes it. Although, in terms of a general theory derived from the philosophical premises of this argument, the basic valuation of Buddhism could be construed as asserting "Nirvana is that with which human beings ought unconditionally to be engaged," the argument itself assumes that "Nirvana" (and related terms in other communities) either stands for or deflects attention from that which ought unconditionally to engage human beings, that is, the Triune God. This assumption is made not on the basis of comparison and contrast between Christian doctrines and Buddhist doctrines but a priori and with reference to all possible basic religious valuations at the center of other schemes of doctrines. In effect, the Christian community proposes the only self-consistent basic religious valuation.

The difficulty here is not simply that religious doctrines always elude full explication (something that would be true of Christian as well as of non-Christian doctrines, as we shall observe in the next section). Nor is a judgment being asserted according to which many non-Christian religious doctrines are appraised as erroneous in what they teach or misguided in what they value or recommend. One could judge this to be the case and still take those doctrines as self-consistent, serious alternatives of which their adherents could give a full account (relatively speaking). No difficulties are posed by these points. Nor is there a difficulty in asserting that Christian doctrines express better what other religious doctrines express only partially. If judgments of this sort proceed case by case, there is nothing inappropriate about dialectical arguments that compare and contrast particular religions with Christianity in order to show the latter's superiority to them in the areas in question.

To put the matter briefly, the difficulty posed by the inclusivist argument we have been considering is that it tries to prove too much. In effect, the theory of religion on which it relies suggests that other religious communities could never give an adequate and self-consistent account of their doctrines. In order to be complete (logically speaking), such an account would always have to include an appeal to the basic valuation of the Christian community. The distinctive basic valuations of non-Christian communities, especially nontheistic ones, could not be consistently acknowledged and debated. In effect, prior to dialogue, the universal claims of Buddhist, Hindu, Muslim, and Judaic communities would be absorbed into the embrace of Christian doctrines. Interreligious conversations would in effect serve the purpose of disclosing Christian-like virtualities in the doctrines of these other communities rather than of entertaining such doctrines as self-consistent alternative teachings about that upon which human life should be focused.

Pluralist patterns of referential argument have the more curious result of introducing a new basic religious valuation into the conversation alongside those advanced by Christian, Judaic, Muslim, Buddhist, and Hindu communities. While inclusivists argue that a Christianly construed "Absolute Mystery" is that upon which all religious patterns of life are focused, some pluralists substitute more religiously indeterminate concepts like "Reality" or "Ultimacy" to interpret otherwise distinctive religious objects. Some pluralists argue that the various foci of worship and quest in the major, soteriologically oriented religious communities represent a focus that transcends them all. In effect, this "interpretation" of what religious communities are about constitutes, logically speaking, an independent religious proposal.

Consider the following remarks of Stanley Samartha. He is concerned to avoid exclusivism. In Samartha's view, "Mystery provides the ontological basis for tolerance, which would otherwise run the risk of becoming uncritical friendliness." What Professor Samartha means by "Mystery" is clear when he states that it is the "transcendent Center that remains always beyond and greater than apprehensions of it or even the sum total of those apprehensions." So much is this case that "Mystery lies beyond the theistic/nontheistic debate." For Professor Samartha, the concept provides the basis for understanding the focal objects of religious worship and quest in religious communities. Thus, in Hinduism and Christianity, respectively, "the terms 'Brahman' and

'God' are culture-conditioned. One could as well use the term Mystery, which may be more acceptable." Distinctive Hindu and Christian doctrines about Brahman and God can be understood as diverse "responses to the same Mystery in two cultural settings." This is true, according to Professor Samartha, of "the two statements . . . that 'Brahman is *sat-cit-ananda* [truth-consciousness-bliss]' and 'God is triune, Father, Son, and Holy Spirit.' . . . At best, the two formulations can only be symbolic, pointing to the Mystery, affirming the meaning disclosed, but retaining residual depth."[13]

The presumption here is that the list of doctrinally specific religious terms pointing to Mystery could be extended beyond Brahman and the Triune God to include the Muslim's Allah, the Jew's Lord God, and the Buddhist's Nirvana. It is a common feature of theological proposals in the pluralist vein to construe the focal objects of communities in this fashion. Terms like "Mystery," "Reality," or "Ultimacy," appear to function as logical equivalents in what seems to be a general theory of religions underlying the pluralist account of distinctive basic valuations. But we can notice in Professor Samartha's remarks that the term "Mystery" functions chiefly not as an equivalent for a predicate value like "that which ought unconditionally to engage human beings" but as a substitute for terms in the place of *m* in basic religious valuations. In effect, on the basis of Professor Samartha's and similar accounts, one could say that "Mystery" or "Reality" is that which ought unconditionally to engage human beings. "Mystery" is that to which basic religious valuations refer when they speak of the focal objects of worship and quest upon which life ought to be centered. Beyond those existents or states lies something that finally eludes reference. Terms like "Mystery," or "Reality," favored by pluralist theologians of religions, function as the actual underlying subject of the various unrestricted primacy-

13. Stanley J. Samartha, "The Cross and the Rainbow," in *The Myth of Christian Uniqueness*, ed. Hick and Knitter, 75–76.

ranking predications assigned by religious communities to God, Brahman, Nirvana, and so on.

In terms of the foregoing analysis, pluralist theology of religions thus seems in effect to import a basic religious valuation under the guise of a general theory of religion. In a general theory, the basic valuation of the Buddhist scheme could be construed as asserting that Nirvana is that with which human beings ought unconditionally to be engaged. But, by implying that there is something beyond Nirvana that engages human beings unconditionally, pluralist theology of religions advances a broadly theistic account of the Buddhist doctrine of Nirvana. This account posits the existence of some entity, "Mystery," with which some engagement, even the vaguest experience, is possible. Yet, according to the logic of Buddhist doctrines, Nirvana refers not to a presently existing object—no matter how impersonally or nontheistically conceived—but to a state of being yet to be realized. The concept of "Mystery" seems to retain unexpungeably presential or existential features that run counter to Buddhist descriptions of Nirvana. By suggesting that "Mystery" lies beyond or behind Nirvana, God, Brahman, and the like, pluralist theology of religions unwittingly gets itself into the position of seeming to advance the only self-consistent basic religious valuation.

This presumably unintended outcome arises because pluralist theology of religions introduces a new basic religious valuation into the conversation alongside those advanced by Christian, Judaic, Muslim, Buddhist, and Hindu communities. Pluralists substitute religiously indeterminate concepts like "Reality" or "Mystery" for otherwise distinctively conceived religious objects (whether they be presently existing entities or yet to be realized states). Pluralists argue that the various foci of worship and quest in the major, soteriologically oriented religious communities represent a focus that finally transcends them all. In effect, this "interpretation" of what religious communities are about constitutes, logically speaking, an independent religious proposal.

Taken as a reading of the particular referential arguments advanced by existing religious communities, the pluralist account construes religious differences about the nature of the objects of worship and quest as ultimately resolvable into a higher synthesis that transcends the reach of the doctrines of all existing religious communities. On this view, interreligious conversations would chiefly occasion, not debate about serious religious alternatives, but disclosure of the cognate soteriological structures of the participating religious communities.

In fact, pluralist accounts of these issues are in part warranted by theories about the nature of religious predications that significantly underrate their assertive force. Let us turn now to a consideration of the logic of arguments in support of predications.

EXPRESSING THE INEXPRESSIBLE

The Triune God whom we worship, Christians say, is holy, good, eternal, all-powerful, merciful, loving, and so on. Indeed, all perfections in their highest degree can be ascribed to him. Such ascriptions are warranted by arguments that combine complex appeals to the Scriptures, to liturgical and doctrinal sources, to common Christian usage in prayer, teaching, and nurture with philosophically framed appeals to objective states of affairs in the world. Once a reference to the Triune God as cause of the world has launched Christian discourse—in theological exposition, in interreligious conversations, or in other settings—then there is room for arguments that support the range of things that Christians believe to be true about him. Patterns of argument that support such predications can be understood to address the question, what kind of life does the cause of the world enjoy?

Aquinas neatly expresses the difficulty such arguments pose for Christian theologians when he frankly states at the start of his own discussion of these matters that "we cannot know what God is, but rather what he is not."[14] It follows that the burden of arguments warranting Christian ascriptions of various primacy-ranking predicates to the Triune God—the so-called divine attributes—consists largely in excluding imperfections from him. In addition, it must be shown that such predications, despite their limitations, do indeed advance truth claims about the Triune God.

Both of these functions of such arguments are relevant to their serviceability in interreligious conversations. Rival and possibly conflicting claims about the reality that ultimately engages human beings are central to the exchange for which such conversations afford the opportunity. Such conversations would lack intellectual seriousness and religious urgency if the predications expressed by the doctrines of participating communities were thought not to bear directly on the nature of this reality. Granted the fundamental ineffability of this reality, major religious communities have concurred in holding that their respective doctrines express the truth about this reality and about humankind's relation to it. Indeed, disagreements among these communities about what this truth is and what its implications are for the shape of human life drew their point from this basic conviction about the force of their doctrines.

In the Christian community, an influential defense of this conviction has been developed by Aquinas in connection with a theory of the analogical character of religious doctrines that express propositions. This theory serves to support predicational patterns of argument in Christian theology. In combination with the referential patterns of argument examined earlier, such arguments have an important role to play in interreligious conversations. Study of Aquinas's account of these arguments helps us to see what is at stake for Christian theology as it embraces such conversations.

Fundamental to Aquinas's account of the logic of predicational

14. Thomas Aquinas, *Summa theologiae*, 1a. 3, prologue.

patterns of argument is his construal of the divine simplicity in terms of the notion of sheer existence.[15] Enjoying the life of the cause of the world entails being sheerly existent (a concept expressed by Aquinas in the phrase, *ipsum esse per se subsistens*), as opposed to everything else that, as caused, enjoys a life that is only derivatively existent. Only that which is sheerly existent can be the cause of what is derivatively existent. Discussion of the divine simplicity provides Aquinas with the opportunity to make this point because, in ruling out composition in God, the attribute of simplicity rules out any potentiality in him, including the most basic potentiality to the actuality of existence. In contrast with all derivatively existent entities—that is, things that receive, and are therefore in potency to, existence—only the Triune God is simply and fully actual. Derivatively existent things are not simple: they are composed, most basically by the actuality of existence and the potentiality for existence. If the Triune God were composed in this way, then something else would be cause of the world or source of the existence of all derivatively existent entities.

It is because the Triune God is sheerly existent in the sense stipulated that our predications fail to encompass him. The difficulty we face in our discourse about God emerges clearly when we notice the grammatical structure of all our predications. They are precisely that, ascriptions of predicates to subjects. The very grammar of our talk about things reflects their "composed" nature as derivatively existent entities. Hence, as Aquinas notes, the mode of signification matches the nature of what is signified. The ascription of various predicates ("smart," "a New Yorker," "skilled at tennis," and so on) to a particular subject ("Jack") reflects the fact that these and many other traits and dispositions come together to constitute this subject. Our predications about God possess the same grammatical structure as our predications about Jack: we say that God is holy, merciful, sheerly existent, and so on. We have no other linguistic forms at our disposal but

15. Thomas Aquinas, *Summa theologiae*, 1a. 3, 4.

these. Yet, in our use of such forms of utterance to speak about God, the mode of signification fails completely to match the nature of what is signified. God just isn't composed in the way that our talk about him suggests. Being holy, being merciful, being sheerly existent, and so on—these are nothing else than being God. Our talk about God draws distinctions where in him no distinctions exist. God is holy, merciful, sheerly existent, and so on, in a way that utterly surpasses our capacities to understand or describe. These capacities are fit for talk about the only things of which we can have direct experience, viz., what is derivatively existent.

Christian theology needs some account of our predications about the Triune God to show that, despite their serious limitations, they nonetheless entail claims to truth. When Christians assert that God is holy, or merciful, or sheerly existent, and acknowledge that they do not know what it is like for God to be these things, they still mean to assert that these predications are true of him. On the face of things, many of the utterances Christians employ in talking about God, in praying to him, in invoking his power, in teaching about him, and in other settings imply an affirmative propositional force.

For this reason, some semantic characterizations of the force of such predictions do not adequately account for what Christians seem to mean by them. Aquinas's proposes his own theory of analogy as an alternative to three such characterizations.[16] The first suggests that all such predications can be reformulated as paradoxical or apophatic utterances that deny limitations to God (thus: "God is good" would be equivalent to "God is not evil"). Another semantic theory of religious predications reconstrues them as assertions about the divine causal activity as experienced by us. What appear on the surface as ascriptions of attributes to the Triune God are in fact construable as descriptions of our experience of him, or of our relation to him (thus: "God is good" is

16. Thomas Aquinas, *Summa theologiae*, 1a. 13.

equivalent to "God is the cause of goodness"). Neither of these theories denies the propositional force of Christian doctrines that express predications. Rather, according to the first view, the propositional force is always negative, while according to the second, it is always relative to human states. There is a third view that seems to exclude the propositional force of predications about the Triune God. According to this view, such predications must be construed as metaphorical, as evocations (nondiscursive symbols) that afford, occasion, or express certain experiences of the transcendent realm without being directly descriptive of it (thus "God is good" is symbolic).

These accounts of the force of religious doctrines are correct as far as they go: the nature of the Triune God transcends the reach of our terms and concepts in their ordinary uses and meanings. But these accounts are partial in that they require an implausible reconstrual of all the straightforwardly affirmative predications that occur throughout the range of Christian usage. Some nonreductive account of such predications is needed, and Aquinas advances the theory of analogy as such an account. There is a conviction that many ordinary concepts are already employed in analogous senses and that, given the proper qualifications, they can be employed in religious and theological discourse.

The theory of analogy thus provides the basis for predicational patterns of argument that both acknowledge their peculiar logical form and allow for their propositional force. The theory of analogy functions as a theory of predication, framed to account for Christian discourse in use, and providing a straightforward reading of utterances that have the form of affirmative predications. Aquinas supports the theory by appealing to philosophical and theological premises. The use of well-developed concepts of being, causality, and participation (the so-called "*analogia entis*") links Christian predications about the Triune God with objective states of affairs and thus reinforces the universal scope that is signaled for such doctrines by referential patterns of argument. Theological premises, particularly concerning creation and the created order, yield the basic context for applying concepts and terms honed in talk about the derivatively existent to talk about that which is sheerly existent.

Aquinas's discussion of human knowledge of God confirms the foregoing reading of the logic of predications about God. In question 12 of the first part of the *Summa theologiae* the bulk of the articles (eleven to be exact) are devoted to the beatific knowledge of God, and only one article each to faith and natural knowledge of God. This disproportionate treatment might be construed as follows. Any adequate description of the range of human knowledge of God in the present life must begin with some account of what our knowledge of him will be like in the life to come. To put this another way: we will grasp the full scope of our capacity to know God now only by considering the consummation toward which our present knowledge is directed by grace. What is possible to us now can be appreciated only in the light of what our knowledge shall become. We are invited to see human knowledge of God from above, as it were, down to its lower levels. It is not so much a matter of independent bodies of knowledge, natural and then revealed, which develop independently and then come to be related to one another. All that is true knowledge is taken up into the knowledge of faith, and that in turn into the knowledge of vision. Everything that is part of human knowing and willing as natural capacities is taken up to function at a higher level, that is, successfully knowing and loving God.

Thus the chief strengths of Aquinas's account of the nature and grace of religious knowledge and the logic of religious predications lies in its capacity to relate Christian affirmations to a wide variety of explanatory contexts beyond their linguistic, narrative, historical, and subjective settings. Such an account breaks through the constraints imposed on Christian theology in the course of its long dialogue with the modern western philosophical tradition. The internal logic of the discourse of religious traditions entails at least the possibility that primary doctrines can be supported by arguments to establish a reference to the entity or state at the center of the community's pattern of life and arguments to explicate the force of its predications.

An account of Christian predications that admits their propositional force would equip Christian theology in dialogue to engage in conversations with other major religious communities. Generally speaking, these communities concur with the Christian community (though accounting for it differently) in claiming objective states of affairs as the context for their teachings about God (if they have any), the true aim of life, and the conditions of human existence in the world. Equipped with an account of the logic of religious predications, such as that inspired by a reading of Aquinas, a Christian theologian would be prepared to take disagreements about these matters seriously. In particular, there are significant disagreements between Muslim and Christian communities about whether the unity of God excludes or permits relations in him, and between Buddhist and Christian communities about whether the ultimate state entails or negates personal identity and interrelationships. These differences are not vacuous, though whether they represent true oppositions is a matter for dialogue and debate among the communities concerned. In effect, an account of the logic of religious predications that admits their propositional force, such as the one provided here, can be read as a defense of the possibility and seriousness of interreligious disagreements and conversation about them.

It is a weakness of pluralist accounts of religious predications that they seem to underrate the fundamental seriousness of such disagreements. We noted above that one warrant for Professor Samartha's introduction of the concept "Mystery" was that the "transcendent Center . . . remains always beyond and greater than apprehensions of it or even the sum total of such apprehensions."[17] It is typical of pluralist accounts of religious predications to stress the ineffability of the transcendent realm and furthermore to argue that differing doctrines about the foci of

17. Stanley J. Samartha, "The Cross and the Rainbow," 75.

religious quest or worship in the major traditions diversely designate something that is itself absolutely indescribable. Behind and beyond the Christian's Triune God, the Jew's Lord God, the Muslim's Allah, the Hindu's Brahman, and the Buddhist's Nirvana, there lies an ineffable "X"—variously identified by pluralist accounts as "Ultimacy," "Reality," or "Mystery"—that itself never appears except in these scheme-specific manifestations. John Hick calls these manifestations "personae."[18]

Ascriptions of ineffability of religious communities to the objects of worship or quest upon which their patterns of life are centered have a variety of functions. Naturally, they have the obvious function of stating that no concepts or expressions can succeed in comprehending that which completely surpasses ordinary experience, sense-perception, and knowledge. But such ascriptions also function as unrestricted primacy-ranking predicates. What is describable and comprehensible is also accessible and therefore similar to other entities within our experience. But the object of worship or quest is normally not thought to be one more item within our experience but either the transcendent source of all there is (as in most theistic traditions) or the goal beyond all there is (as in some nontheistic traditions). An indication of this function is that in the literatures of the Buddhist and Christian communities respectively, for example, affirmations of the utter ineffability of Nirvana or the Triune God are juxtaposed to extensive descriptions of what Nirvana entails and what the nature of God is like. To combine ineffability with other unrestricted primacy-ranking predicates like most holy, or perfectly good, or supreme goal of life, is to acknowledge the limitations of all discourse that seeks to speak about that which transcends human knowledge and speech. But from the ineffability of the transcendent realm it does not follow for either Buddhists or Christians that certain forms of predications about it are not

18. John Hick, *An Interpretation of Religion: Human Responses to the Transcendent* (New Haven: Yale University Press, 1989), 233–96.

more appropriate than others, or that particular forms of predications are not ruled out, or that in some way these communities' authorized ways of speaking about Nirvana and God do not bear on the truth of the matter. In other words, predicate-expressing doctrines do possess some propositional force.

For this reason, the members of these communities generally believe that some real disagreements obtain between them. Buddhists, for example, have developed highly sophisticated accounts for the prevalence of theistic beliefs. An account of religious predications that admits their propositional force, though it does not deny their limitations, is basic to interreligious dialogue. Generally speaking, as we have noted, the major religious communities of the world agree in identifying objective states of affairs as the context for their teachings about God, the true aim of life, the conditions of human existence in the world, and so on. This conviction gives rise to arguments that seek to secure each community's particularistic claim to universality. An account of religious predications that admits their propositional force (without denying their negative, rulish, symbolic, or metaphorical functions) is presupposed if disagreements among religious communities are to be taken seriously. There are significant disagreements between Muslim, Jewish, and Christian communities about the nature of divine unity, and between Buddhist and Christian communities about whether personal identity and personal interrelationships are ultimately enduring. These differences are significant, although to what extent they constitute real oppositions is a matter of reflection, dialogue, and debate. In effect, an account of the logic of religious predications that admits their propositional force takes the possibility of interreligious disagreements seriously.

In its familiar versions, pluralist theology of religions seems to hold a view of religious predications that sharply qualifies their propositional force. The logic of pluralist accounts seems to entail that no predicate-expressing doctrines of one religious community could ever be said to embody descriptions bearing on the true nature of the ineffable "X" such as to conflict with or rule out predications expressed in the doctrines of other religious communities. Furthermore, the chief function (logically speaking) of doctrinally specific arguments for the primary predications by which religious communities identify their objects of worship or quest would be to converge upon and point to the "Mystery" or "Reality" that eludes them all.

Pluralist accounts of religious predications are reminiscent of modalistic explanations of the Christian doctrine of the Trinity. It will be recalled that the modalism that spurred doctrinal controversy in the early church involved some version of the view that "Father, Son, and Holy Spirit" designate roles or "personae" adopted by God in executing various stages of the economy of salvation. The historic mainstream repudiated this view by affirming the reality of the distinct relations in God as warranted by the scriptural witness to the real processions of the Son and the Spirit. In effect, in rejecting modalistic explanations of the doctrine of the Trinity, the Christian community took "Father, Son, and Holy Spirit" to constitute the substance of a divine self-identification. Anything less was understood to amount to a retrogression to the sophisticated philosophical interpretations of pagan polytheism according to which the gods were viewed as so many diverse manifestations of a single transcendent divine spirit. If "Father, Son and Holy Spirit" represent only modes of God's engagement with humankind, then it would follow that God in himself remains unknown. His true identity is hidden from human view behind the "personae" he displays for soteriological or other purposes. For modalism, "Father, Son and Holy Spirit" finally constitute a practiced concealment rather than, as the Gospel was understood to proclaim, a full disclosure of God's identity and purposes.

Pluralist positions are equivalently modalistic in their account of the logic of religious predications. In the current "neomodalism" of pluralist theology of religions, the diverse doctrines by which each religious community designates the otherwise ineffable "X" (Nirvana, the Blessed Trinity, Allah, etc.) embody only partial and possibly complementary descriptions of something that finally eludes them all.

Suppose that a well-informed but non-affiliated inquirer is welcomed as an observer into a dialogue with members of Judaic, Christian, Muslim, and Buddhist communities. He is permitted an intervention, and in the course of speaking announces that either Christianity is true, or Buddhism is true, or no religion is true. His argument for this ferociously contentious claim is not without interest. It takes its starting point from the importance of personal identity and interpersonal relationships among human beings. Christian doctrines, as he understands them, affirm the centrality of these relationships to the extent that person and relation are ascribed even to God himself. That which is most important to human beings, their self-fulfillment in the context of intimate relations with other persons, turns out to be most important in the transcendent realm as well. As he construes it, the doctrine of the Trinity allows for the possibility that human beings can be intimately related to God in a truly interpersonal way. He understands this possibility to be excluded by nontrinitarian theistic faiths, which allow only for worship of or submission to God. Buddhist doctrines, on the other hand, seem to him to assert the illusoriness of personal identity and the impermanence of interpersonal relationships. Thus he concludes that since Christian and Buddhist doctrines both take into account observably central features of the objective states of human existence in the world, and advance predications about what is ultimate that reflect these features, they have a greater truth potential than religious doctrines failing to do so.

On the pluralist account of religious predications, it is hard to see how responses from the religious participants in such a conversation could amount to anything for or against this complex interpretation of their doctrines. If religious doctrines expressing predications are in principle construed as failing to assert anything definitive about that which is transcendent, then there is no point in debating the truth of religious doctrines expressing contradictory or even just different accounts of it. Moreover, there are no reasonable grounds, all things being equal, upon which to prefer one community's pattern of life to another's. The very inquiry about such matters loses urgency, and interreligious conversations are rendered finally otiose. Such an outcome runs counter to the deepest convictions with which religious communities commend their doctrines and the patterns of life they foster. Generally speaking, pluralist accounts of religious predications appear to attenuate the significance of religious differences in the course of trying to account for them.

It has been argued in this chapter that traditional philosophical theology equips Christian theology in dialogue with a conception of the logic of religious references and predications that is well suited to the challenge of the encounter with other religions. There is wide scope for referential and predicational arguments in interreligious conversations. Christian theology in dialogue is in effect invited by its new conversation partners in the great world religions to recover and reconstruct arguments of this kind. Such arguments stake a claim, logically speaking, in the large territory of human knowledge about the world. There are no internal restrictions that prevent the appeal of such arguments to relevant scientific findings or to metaphysical and conceptual analysis. The Kantian critique of metaphysics and natural theology continues mistakenly to be invoked in support of such constraints. The mistake here is the failure to recognize that the pervasive rationalism of Kant's conceptions of epistemology and metaphysics is itself susceptible of counterargument and revision. In effect, whatever their other weaknesses, nonrationalist metaphysical positions (Aristotle's for example) escape unscathed. As accounts of the discourse of religious traditions, philosophical theories that rule out in principle a broadly realist construal of religious predications will seem implausible and counterintuitive. As far as the logic of the discourse of religious communities is concerned, the burden of proof lies with these theories themselves.

In addition, the recovery of a philosophical theology such as that sketched here avoids some of the pitfalls associated with projects labeled "fundamental theology" or "foundational theology." Attention to the logic of arguments that support references and predications and thus secure the universal scope claimed by the Christian community for its doctrines does not commit Christian theology in dialogue to the discredited Cartesian project of grounding the certitude of all knowledge in unassailably true, simple, lapidary propositions or conceptions. "Foundational theology" has come to be linked with neoscholastic apologetics of a rationalist cast or with the more recent transcendental project of explicating the truth of Christian doctrines in terms of the conditions for the possibility of our knowledge of them. The proposal of a role for arguments in support of the references and predications embedded in Christian affirmations is a much more modest one. Philosophical theology, according to this account, does not seek to ground the truth of these affirmations, but locates the widest possible context for our understanding and explication of them. It resists the suggestion that these affirmations apply only in the narrow contexts defined by subjectivity, historical consciousness, or language. Staking this claim is not equivalent to establishing a foundation for the truth of all Christian doctrines once and for all. That "foundation" exists only in the truth who is God himself and can never be a human construction. Rather, the readiness to develop and employ arguments of the sort described here characterizes a conception of the theological enterprise in which—case by case, doctrine by doctrine—the force of Christian affirmations is expounded in connection with the full range of human knowledge of the world. The label "foundational theology" is taken to designate, rightly or wrongly, a project far more grand than the one in view in this chapter.

Arguments that support references and predications function

to locate Christian affirmations about the nature and existence of God, his inner-trinitarian life, creation, revelation and grace, human nature, sin and evil, incarnation and redemption, justification and sanctification, morality and spirituality, Church and sacraments, resurrection and glory, eschatology and the last things in the widest possible context of reality, thought, and experience. In this way, such arguments have an important role to play in interreligious conversations, where Christians encounter in the doctrines of other communities the challenge of similarly particularistic claims to universality. Philosophical theology helps Christian theology in dialogue to rise to this challenge.

CHAPTER FIVE

Conclusion

MANY AN explorer has been lost because of inaccurate maps, or inexperienced guides, or other unforeseen mishaps. Most unfortunate of all has been the fate of one who was lost from the very beginning for having started off in the wrong direction. On the assumption that the doctrines of other religious communities could somehow be taken into account in developing proposals in Christian theology of religions, the foregoing chapters have been exploring the terrain beyond the limits of current debate. Could this assumption have gotten our inquiry off to a bad start?

For one thing, how could a Christian theologian acquire a sufficient mastery of the doctrines of even one other religious community such that he could bring this knowledge effectively into play in theology of other religions? Phra Khantipalo's warning comes to mind at this juncture: "So complex, so intricate is the Dharma, that researches into it can only be fully successful by those who are themselves constantly applying Buddhadharma to their own lives and have thereby developed their own insight. Non-Buddhists investigating Buddhism are almost certain to blunder somewhere."[1] This comment alerts the Christian theologian to just one of the perils that lie in wait when he seeks to take account of Buddhist doctrines (and other communities' as well) in the construction of proposals in theology of religions.

1. Phra Khantipalo, *Tolerance: A Study from Buddhist Sources* (London: Rider & Company, 1964), 139.

But perhaps more serious is the possibility that our inquiry has from the outset misconceived the nature of inquiries in Christian theology of religions. The foregoing chapters seem to have argued that neglect of other religions is a serious deficiency in a discipline whose main purpose is to provide some account of the alternative patterns of life fostered by non-Christian religious communities. An exclusively dogmatic or innerly Christian account of other religions—whatever its advantages for disclosing the logic of central Christian doctrines—could not be relied upon to yield a Christian theology of religions that could do justice to what the adherents of other religions might have to say in proposing their own doctrines.

It might be objected that, if this is the burden of the argument of preceding chapters, then it seems badly misguided. In the first place, it might well be urged that, far from being a deficiency, the generality of standard forms of Christian theology of religions constitutes one of their strongest features. In view of the spectacular diversity of religious claims, the comprehensiveness necessary in a theology of religions depends on its capacity to cover a wide range of possibilities. Its ability to do so could be seriously compromised by detailed consideration of particular religious doctrines and patterns of life, even if a given theologian had acquired a mastery of the study of religions sufficient for such considerations.

Furthermore, it might be argued, the complaint that standard theology of religions for the most part neglects the doctrines of other religious communities involves a confusion about the logic of religious doctrines. Even a Christian theologian well versed in the doctrines of some other religious community would not be competent to speak as one of its members in discussing its doctrines. His theology of religions, where it depended on the mention of the doctrines of some other community, would be vulnerable to objections by members of that community (and others) to the effect that he had misstated or misconstrued its doctrines or that he had mistaken merely permitted opinions for doctrines in that community. His status as a nonmember would render him incompetent to decide in matters of internal dispute which sentences did and which did not correctly express the doctrines of that community. These are some of the blunders against which Phra Khantipalo cautions non-Buddhist interpreters of Buddhist doctrines. Objections citing a Christian theologian's lack of competence or knowledge with regard to the doctrines of other religious communities would possess considerable logical force. If they could be sustained against a particular theology of religions, its plausibility and usefulness would be significantly diminished.

The generality of standard Christian theology of religions might be defended on other grounds as well. It might be argued that such a theology is primarily intended to address issues that arise when Christians want to affirm their faith that other religious people can attain salvation. In a Catholic setting this means demonstrating the possibility of the attainment of a specifically supernatural destiny by persons who are without public access to the supernatural means of grace available in the Christian community. One of the main achievements of standard Christian theology of religions—particularly in its inclusivist versions—is convincingly to have demonstrated this possibility on the basis of unimpeachably traditional dogmatic and theological principles. Surely it is a mistake to fault standard theology of religions for failing to achieve what its exponents do not undertake to achieve: a detailed account of the distinctive doctrines and patterns of life of other religious communities.

In fact, our inquiry has striven to trace a pathway that skirts the major sources of trouble identified by the foregoing set of objections. As to the illustrations drawn from Buddhist doctrines, it can only be hoped that they have been plausible and that the construals of Buddhist literature successful. More importantly, in order to avoid the blunders against which Khantipalo alerts us, the illustrations have been cast in a hypothetical mode. It is no part of the argument of this book to offer a Christian appraisal of the Buddhist tradition, or an account of the possible range of

Christian-Buddhist encounters as such. Indeed, the force of the appeal to illustrations drawn from Buddhist sources or suggested by them does not depend logically on the adequacy of such descriptions and readings of the doctrines and literature of Buddhist communities. Rather, the role of these illustrations in the foregoing inquiry is hypothetical. Given the reasonable supposition that the Christian community will have occasion to encounter religious communities whose doctrines will manifest distinctive claims about the true aim of life (such as those suggested by a plausible construal of the meaning and force of some Buddhist doctrines), then Christian theology of religions should be so constructed as to take account of such claims.

Thus, information drawn from the study of other religious traditions is relevant to this inquiry in the following way. A Christian theologian can offer only what he hopes will be plausible examples of the doctrines of other religious communities that would be relevant to the formulation of Christian doctrines about other religions. With these illustrations in view in his theology of religions, his conclusions would have a hypothetical character: if Christians have occasion to interact (in dialogue or in other settings) with religious communities whose doctrines manifest the features he adduces, then Christian doctrines about other religions should be formulated in ways that will do justice to these doctrines. In proposing that Christian theology of religions take this course, the preceding chapters advance an argument about the nature of the theological task, given the Christian community's determination to pursue a policy of dialogue in its relations with other religious communities.

It is crucial to this argument that the illustrations of Buddhist doctrines be construed as possessing not simply informative but primarily assertive force. The Christian theologian who undertakes inquiries in these areas needs not only to be well informed about the history and institutions of (some) other religious communities, but also to recognize that the doctrines he studies have theological relevance precisely as beliefs proposed for acceptance and courses of action recommended for adoption. The prospect of engagement in interreligious dialogue looms on the horizon, logically speaking. In dialogue, participants not only inform others about their doctrines but also propose them as true and right. This is the point of noting that particularistic claims to universality are embedded in the doctrinal schemes of major religious communities. Thus, it should be noticed in passing that the viewpoint on other religions adopted by Christian theology of religions as it is understood here is different from that of the scientific study of religions. Christian theology of religions also differs from theology of the history of religions, which might employ concepts drawn from the comparative study of religions to illumine or develop Christian doctrines. Logically speaking, the embrace of interreligious dialogue entails that other religious doctrines be entertained as alternative (even if not opposed) proposals encompassing the same general field to which Christian doctrines are understood to apply and as defensible by arguments of various kinds.

A Christian theologian persuaded of the importance of taking other religious doctrines specifically into account when constructing theology of religions would quit the hypothetical mode, of course, if he undertook to practice theology of religions with other communities specifically in view. He would begin developing and proposing doctrines about the doctrines of some other religious community. Our inquiry is meant to demonstrate the interest and viability of such an approach, and thus to invite theologians to think in a new way about the issues posed by theology of religions.

It is not a consequence of the argument advanced in this book that the only valid form of Christian theology of religions in present circumstances is one that moves directly toward the development of doctrines about the doctrines of specific religious communities. There is plenty of warrant in Christian tradition for a theology of religions to remain at a general level. A Christian theologian could be persuaded of the importance of taking other religious doctrines into account but nonetheless develop his position in a general way. There might be good reasons for adopting such a course. A theologian might not feel competent to venture into consideration of the specific doctrines of some other community yet might be compelled to bear witness in his proposals to the Christian confession of confidence in God's universal salvific will and in his action in inspiring truth and rightness in non-Christian beliefs and ways of life. In such a theology of religions, references to alien religious doctrines could possess a hypothetical cast and thus avoid inappropriate or improperly focused uses of Buddhist and other doctrines. Proposals here would be advanced in such a way as to remain systematically open to developments that might be required if specific doctrines of other religious communities actually came to be entertained in dialogue or other settings. A theology of religions in this vein would be sufficiently general and well within the bounds of its competence as a product of reflection within the Christian community, yet it would still be fit to rise to the challenges posed by engagement in interreligious dialogue.

It does follow from the argument of this book that a Christian theology of religions that was not at least open to such developments (logically speaking) would be deficient. This defect would be evident if its proposals were found to be inapplicable to the doctrines of existing religious communities, or in principle to exclude reference to the doctrines of these communities, or systematically to underrate their significance for the formulation of Christian doctrines about other religions. Thus, it would be a sign that a particular theology of religions could serve exclusively internal (or at any rate "nondialogical") purposes if specific referents could never plausibly be substituted for the terms "other religions" and "members of other religious communities" in its main formulations of Christian doctrines about other religions.

It by no means follows from the argument of preceding chapters that a Christian valuation (that is, one framed in Christian categories) of other religions is inappropriate. What else would a properly Christian theology of religions be competent to enunciate but appraisals of other religions framed in Christian terms? This book argues that such appraisals be advanced so that the distinctive claims that other religious doctrines embody either could be or actually are taken into account. Furthermore, in this connection, the approach advocated here does not rule out the possibility that a Christian (or other observer, for that matter) might have a better understanding of what is going on in a religious community than some of its own members do. There is no absolute rule in the religious or in other realms against interpreting the activities or beliefs of other agents or groups of agents in ways that run counter to their self-understanding or self-descriptions. Indeed, respect for them as fellow human beings or as fellow seekers might on some occasions require us to be truthful about what we perceive in their patterns of action and belief. Interreligious dialogue might well provide an occasion of this sort. Thus, in particular cases, it might be correct to assert that another religious community did in fact seem to be bent on attaining what Christians understand salvation to involve, and to adduce specific doctrines in that community as evidence for this assertion. The argument of this book does not rule out such possibilities. It does, however, raise questions about the appropriateness of blanket assertions of this kind that fail to attend to the fact that, at least initially, the self-descriptions of most other religious communities involve distinctive and possibly opposed conceptions of the true aim of life. In addition, it proposes an alternative approach to Christian theology of religions that systematically admits the relevance of such self-descriptions but does not preclude the fielding of counterdescriptions framed in Christian terms.

Current debate in theology of religions, especially in Catholic circles, got its impetus largely from the Second Vatican Council. In general, the participants in this debate have been concerned more to appropriate the council's favorable estimate of the salvific character of other religious communities than to explore the implications of its embrace of interreligious dialogue. In part, the argument of this book strives to redress the balance in interpretation of the conciliar teaching on non-Christian religions. In effect, it seeks to join two forms of discussion that often proceed independently of each other in Christian circles: that in which theological proposals of Christian doctrines about other religions are generated and that in which specific forms of interaction with other religious communities are considered. The suggestion here is that Christian theology of religions be developed, more explicitly than has been the case in the recent past, with the requirements of various forms of interaction, especially interreligious dialogue, in view.

By teaching that God's will to save embraces all human beings, Christian primary doctrines provide the basis for the supposition that the community's doctrines about other religions could account for the salvation of persons who—because they are members not of the visible Christian community but of non-Christian communities—do not have public access to the means of grace. Christian theology of religions endeavors to articulate this supposition in all its dimensions.

What is more, by teaching its members to engage in dialogue with the members of other religious communities, the Christian community can be understood to suppose this practical doctrine about other religions to be consistent with its other doctrines in their regard. In order to elucidate the "logic" of this supposition, we considered in chapter 1 a set of working formulations that summarize traditional Christian doctrines about other religions. The courses of action ingredient in the activity of engaging in dialogue seem to suppose a situation in which, among other things, the doctrines of particular religious communities would be proposed and argued for by their members. It follows that to recommend that their members engage in dialogue, Christian communities suppose that their doctrines about other religions could develop into doctrines about the doctrines of other religions.

Supplementary historical considerations serve to confirm the reasonableness of this supposition. After all, Christian doctrines about other religions started out as doctrines about particular religions: first about Judaism, then about other religions and religious philosophies in late antiquity. The fact that such doctrines often came to be invoked subsequently in periods of limited religious interaction with little reference to alien traditions is no reason why these doctrines could not be applied to particular existing religious communities as interaction with them developed. Religious communities typically approach new situations with an eye to their traditional resources. Thus, logically speaking, the recommendation to engage in dialogue supposes that Christian doctrines about other religions could be formulated to do justice to the distinctive claims advanced by the adherents of traditions with whom dialogue is envisaged. Part of the task of theology of religions in present circumstances is to develop traditional Christian doctrines about other religions along these lines.

For various reasons, prevailing positions within the field of Christian theology of religions seem ill-equipped for this task. Their common espousal of what we have called the soteriocentric principle tends to obscure for pluralists and inclusivists alike the varieties of aims commended and pursued by the Hindu, Buddhist, Muslim, and Judaic communities. The central objective of pluralists and inclusivists is to allow for the possibility of salvation outside the confines of the Christian community. Their considerable disagreements arise from the alternative theological and philosophical strategies they deploy in pursuing that objective. Fundamental to this endeavor is the soteriocentric principle according to which all religious communities aim for salvation either as Christians understand it (inclusivism) or in the various forms in which it comes to be expressed (pluralism).

Given the determination on the part of many theologians to avoid exclusivism in any form, the exclusivist/inclusivist/pluralist typology can best be understood if it is visualized, not as a continuum of positions, but as a trajectory away from exclusivism. This accounts for considerable fluidity in the application of this typology to competing positions. Thus, although inclusivists reject exclusivism, it is not unusual to find pluralists labeling as exclusivist even the mildest inclusivist forms of affirmation of the centrality of Christ for salvation. In pursuing their flight from exclusivism, pluralists are prepared to approach the outer limits of recognizably Christian confession on a range of topics from the doctrine of God and the Trinity, through christology and grace, and on to ecclesiology and sacramental theology.

There is much that is valuable in the vast literature spawned by the debate between pluralists and inclusivists. But it is fast becoming a largely reiterative conversation about familiar proposals. It is a sign of this that new books in the field devote a disproportionately large amount of attention to rehearsing the various alternatives in the field and a relatively small measure of space to proposing their authors' own constructive proposals.

In part, this book has argued for a change of venue, a fresh context for airing these issues, in order to move beyond the current impasse in theology of religions. Two suggestions are central to this argument. In the first place, it needs to be recognized that the alleged "exclusiveness" of traditional Christian doctrines is an expression of a particularistic claim to universality, with cognates in other religious traditions. Christian theology of religions requires an analysis of the particularistic claims to universality that seems to be embedded in the doctrinal schemes of major religious communities. One way of getting at this point is to study the logic of doctrines in religious communities about other religions. A community's concern for the fate of nonmembers and for the value of the religious doctrines they hold and follow is expressed, normally, in its own doctrines about other religions. The seriousness with which a religious community regards the true aim of life and the means by which it can be reliably sought and attained provides the stimulus for such doctrines. Rather than abandon or reconstrue the Christian version of this claim, theology of religions needs to develop an account of its "logic" that will be useful in understanding and appraising analogous claims on the part of the communities encountered in dialogue.

Second, the debate will in all likelihood continually traverse the same pathways unless the soteriocentric framework is qualified or displaced as a way of conceiving the issues. Christian theology of religions needs to grasp the significance of the fact that religious communities actually propose distinctive aims for human life, in which soteriological doctrines have varying degrees of significance and varying sorts of affinities with Christian doctrines about salvation. As was suggested earlier in this chapter, such issues can be sorted out only on the basis of a case by case analysis of the doctrines of other religious communities.

To offset possible misunderstandings of what has been proposed in correcting the soteriocentric principle, it should be noted that it is no part of the argument that having an "aim of life"—whether ultimate or intermediary—is a defining feature of "religion." Nor has it been argued that, within worldwide communities, a single, invariant conception of the true aim of life prevails in all subcommunities. The argument here does entail the observation that "aims of life" figure prominently in existing religious communities and the supposition that, if they exhibit roughly the structure sketched here, then Christian theology of religions should take them into account in advancing proposals about the availability of salvation beyond the confines of the Christian community.

It would be desirable for Christian theologians to develop doctrinally specific accounts, not only of distinctive aims and patterns of life, but also of the sources of truth and rightness in non-Christian religious communities and of the morally upright and religiously estimable dispositions of their members. A preference for doctrinally specific accounts would not preclude the adoption of Christian evaluations of such aspects of the diversely featured religious world that Christians encounter. But it would invest such valuations with a much-needed point of reference in the characteristic self-descriptions and dispositional traits associated with and cultivated in Hindu, Buddhist, Muslim, and Judaic communities. In chapter 3, the notions of the providential diversity of religions and the prospective salvation of their adherents suggest an approach to other religious communities that both expresses esteem for them and fits Christians for participation in dialogue with them. Even if these suggestions turn out to be unpersuasive or inadequate, they nonetheless point Christian theology of religions in the right direction.

It cannot have escaped the notice of the attentive reader that, via the notion of prospective salvation, some form of inclusivism has crept into an account professing to have moved beyond it. One reason for this surely is that the inclusivist alternative exerts a powerful attraction on all Christian theology of religions. Certainly a modest form of inclusivism that allows for the operation of divine grace in all human hearts is unobjectionable in the perspective of the argument of this book. We have seen that it is a fundamental conviction of the Christian faith that wherever salvation occurs—wherever the true aim of life is attained—it is always through the grace of Jesus Christ. But in some of the robust forms of inclusivism that have emerged in recent years, theologians seem to want to claim something more. They want to argue that the members of other religious communities can attain salvation through the exercise of their own religions. It is this additional claim that provokes the critique of inclusivism basic to the argument of this book. The notion of prospective salvation has been offered precisely to override this additional claim without denying the unassailable Christian principle entailed in more modest forms of inclusivism.

The willingness to participate in dialogue—indeed, given present circumstances, the inevitability of having to do so—requires not only that Christian theology of religions take the doctrinal claims and arguments of other communities seriously, but that theology in dialogue be prepared to develop and propose Christian arguments that are serviceable in interreligious conversations. This objective presumes the viability and reconstruction of referential and predicational patterns of argument, geared to match the forms of argument advanced by other communities in support of their particularistic claims to universality. The various traditions of Christian philosophical theology have an important role to play at least in launching such arguments. Other religious communities represent rather more challenging dialogue partners for the Christian community than does skeptical philosophy. Their doctrines advance highly ramified and communally legitimated alternative conceptions touching on all aspects of the pursuit, attainment, and enjoyment of the true aim of life. As far as the level of conversation and the aptitudes of the participants are concerned, one could say that in every respect the conversation partners are well matched.

Although it has fallen outside the scope of this book to argue the case, the theology of religions sketched here is fully compatible with a strong affirmation of Christian mission. The determination on the part of the Christian community to respect the particularistic claims to universality advanced by other communities is paralleled by its own conviction about the universal scope of salvation in Jesus Christ. As Pope John Paul II has recently written: "While respecting the beliefs and sensitivities of all, we must first clearly affirm our faith in Christ, the one Savior of humanity, a faith we have received as a gift from on high, not as a result of any merit of our own."[2]

The approach to theology of religions advocated in these chapters would permit arguments by Christian participants in dialogue, or by Christian missionaries, to the effect that the aims of life commended by other communities inadequately or erroneously or misguidedly envisage the true aim of life that the Christian community strives to commend and foster in fidelity to its risen Lord. The approach suggested here has advantages over inclusivist and pluralist positions for legitimating engagement in evangelization. For many inclusivists, the Christian mission comes to be viewed primarily as the identification of virtualities

2. *Redemptoris Missio:* On the Permanent Validity of the Church's Missionary Mandate, para. 11 (Boston: St. Paul Books, 1990), 20.

already present in other religions, or as the explicitation and arousal of inclinations already implicit in the dispositions of their adherents. Although, naturally, inclusivist theology of missions envisages the correction and fulfillment of non-Christian practices and beliefs, it nonetheless fails to sustain the urgency toward proclamation that traditional Christian doctrines have been understood to entail. The logic of pluralist positions, on the other hand, seems to preclude anything but the mildest forms of specifically Christian witness. Pluralist theology of mission would be concerned to advocate forms of collaboration with non-Christian communities in projects expressing common human concern to alleviate the plight of those in need and to address larger social and political injustices.

It seems clear, however, that the traditional Christian policy of evangelization and mission has something more vigorous in view. Neither inclusivist nor pluralist approaches to the theology of mission have been successful in summoning the energies of the Christian communities in which they are dominant for exercise in the field of evangelization. It is a commonplace to note the contrast of these views of mission with those of communities in which more exclusivist forms of theology of religions predominate. But the foregoing chapters suggest that engagement in Christian mission can be fully legitimated by nonexclusivist doctrinal and theological strategies. A vigorous Christian mission presupposes convictions about the particularity of the hope for and the universality of the scope of the salvation about which Christians are charged to bear witness. Esteem for other religious communities and respect for their members do not preclude engagement in this mission, even if they do entail the abandonment of some of the practices associated with missionary activity in the past.

Consider one final objection to the approach advocated in this book. If, as Christians, we believe in the unity of humankind and the singleness of God's purposes in its regard, then surely one of the objectives of Christian theology of religions would be to gain and to promote an awareness of this unity in our beliefs and practices across the relatively artificial boundaries of rival religious communities. The distinguished British physicist Paul Davies wrote recently: "Few would deny that religion remains, for all its pretensions, one of the most divisive forces in society."[3] There is always the danger of rekindling the bitter religious conflicts that have plagued humankind throughout history and continue to haunt the human race in our own day. It hardly seems appropriate under the circumstances to advocate a theological approach to these issues that accentuates rather than minimizes religious differences.

Such sentiments rightly caution Christian theologians of religions against making too much of religious differences. The pitfalls of arrogance and intolerance lie in wait for the unsuspecting inquirer who travels these paths. Still, recognizing differences is not equivalent to promoting discord. It is a way of taking other religious people seriously. In an important study of religious tolerance, the philosopher Jay Newman has written: "The teachings of Judaism and Christianity, Buddhism and Islam, Catholicism and Methodism, are, though significantly similar in many areas, far from identical. If religious creeds are worth taking seriously, then the differences between one creed and another are worth taking seriously."[4] Frank acknowledgment of the diversity of religions is fully consonant with attitudes of religious tolerance. Indeed, as Newman argues, since religious tolerance involves an attitude of mind in which one resolves to bear with religious positions that one does not accept, it presupposes the reality and import of differences in religious doctrines.

Without denying its biological and ontological bases, the unity of humankind is part of the eschatological prospect seen here as

3. Paul Davies, *God and the New Physics* (New York: Simon & Schuster, 1983), 4.

4. Jay Newman, *Foundations of Religious Tolerance* (Toronto: University of Toronto Press, 1982), 55.

a hope held out for the whole human race by the Christian community. Christians believe that the unity of humankind is now partly obscured and unrealized, but that in the end humankind will be one with itself and with the Triune God. Moreover, knowledge of the promise and hope for its consummation depend, at least in part, on Christian fidelity to the narration and sacramental re-enactment of the particular events in which this promise was proclaimed, its hope confirmed, and its consummation assured.

Regrettably, human beings are often at odds with one another. Only in the final victory of the cross that is the prelude to glory will the differences—including religious differences—now dividing humankind be healed of their destructive potential. This book has registered a "plea for the recognition of differences."[5] A theology of religions that assumes the religious unity of humankind by dissolving rather than resolving religious differences seeks prematurely to enjoy an eschatological promise whose fulfillment will come only as a stunning and undeserved gift.

The object of this book has been to invite theologians and other concerned Christians to take a fresh look at the issues posed for the Christian community by current circumstances of religious interaction. The style has been deliberately exploratory and hypothetical. At various points in the foregoing chapters, the reader has been invited to inch along a frontier and then to move beyond it. The possibility of returning to the more entrenched and familiar forms of discourse represented by many inclusivist and pluralist positions remains open. But there is also the possibility that the territory beyond the boundaries of current debate may afford opportunities for theological construction not otherwise envisaged. This discovery would count as a good reason for not turning back.

5. Steven T. Katz, "Language, Epistemology and Mysticism," in *Mysticism and Philosophical Analysis,* ed. Steven T. Katz (New York: Oxford University Press, 1978), 25.

Bibliographical Notes

The following notes reflect only the literature that has had a direct role in shaping the argument of this book, chapter by chapter, either by supporting or illustrating aspects of the argument, or by presenting alternative positions. There is no attempt to provide a complete survey of the relevant literature in the theology of religions. However, some bibliographical aids are mentioned below.

CHAPTER ONE: CHRISTIAN DOCTRINES ABOUT OTHER RELIGIONS

In order to adopt a doctrinally specific viewpoint on religious differences, the Christian theologian needs to have some knowledge of religious traditions other than his own. Gaining an adequate knowledge of even one religious tradition and employing it properly are tasks that pose considerable challenges. For a discussion of this challenge, see Francis X. Clooney, Paul J. Griffiths, Charles Hallisey, and James Laine, "Catholic Theology and the Study of Religion in South Asia," *Theological Studies* 48 (1987), 677–710.

At various points in this book, the argument has been supported or key issues illustrated by reference to Buddhist scriptures and literature. In addition to sources directly cited in the footnotes, several works have been particularly helpful in shaping the discussion of the doctrines of the Buddhist community: Frank E. Reynolds, "Buddhism," in *A Reader's Guide to the Great Religions,* ed. Charles J. Adams (New York: The Free Press, 1977), 156–221; Edward Conze, *A Short History of Buddhism* (London: George Allen & Unwin, 1980); Christmas Humphreys, *A Popular Dictionary of Buddhism* (London: Curzon Press, 1976); Winston L. King, *In the Hope of Nibbana: The Ethics of Theravada Buddhism* (LaSalle, Illinois: Open Court Press, 1964); Walpola Rahula, *What the Buddha Taught* (New York: Grove Press, 1974); D. T. Suzuki, *The Essence of Buddhism* (London: The Buddhist Society, 1947); S. Tachibana, *The Ethics of Buddhism* (London: Curzon Press, 1975); A. K. Warder, *Indian Buddhism* (Delhi: Motilal Banarsidass, 1970).

The discussion throughout this chapter presupposes and develops an account of the logic of religious doctrines dependent upon several works in the philosophy of religion: J. M. Bochenski's *The Logic of Religion* (New York: New York University Press, 1965); Ninian Smart's *Reasons and Faiths* (London: Routledge & Kegan Paul, 1958); and especially William A. Christian's *Meaning and Truth in Religion* (Princeton: Princeton University Press, 1964); *Opposition of Religious Doctrines* (New York: Seabury, 1972); "Bochenski on the Structure of Schemes of Doctrines," *Religious Studies* 13 (1977), 203–19; and *Doctrines of Religious Communities: A Philosophical Study* (New Haven: Yale University Press, 1987). William Christian's philosophical analysis of the logic of religious doctrines and arguments is fundamental to the account of theology of religions advanced in this book.

In the last-mentioned book, William Christian discusses doctrines about the doctrines of other religions, but there is as yet no broad philosophical account of "doctrines about other religions" beyond the one sketched in this chapter and presented earlier in a more technical form in J. A. DiNoia, "The Doctrines of a Religious Community about Other Religions," *Religious Studies* 18 (1983), 293–307. An important strand in the argument of this book is that analysis of some general features of the logic of such doctrines brings a much-needed perspective to the study of Christian theology of religions. In the light of an analysis of the logic of doctrines about other religions, the alleged "exclusiveness" of traditional Christian views of other religions can be recognized as an expression of the Christian community's particularistic claim to universality, a claim that has analogues in the discourse of other major religious communities as well. In a religious community, doctrines about other religions arise in part precisely to assess other communities in the light of this claim.

A more complete philosophical analysis of the logic of doctrines about other religions would have been beyond the scope of the argument of this book. In point of fact, the literatures of the world's major religious communities offer a wide field for such study. In addition to the Christian and Buddhist writings mentioned at various points in the course of this book, the following titles suggest something of the potential range and interest of the subject: Muhammad Hamidullah, "Status of Non-Muslims in Islam," *Majallat al Azhar* 45 (1973), no. 8, 6–13; no. 9, 12–16; Neal Robinson, *Christ in Islam and Christianity* (Albany: State University of New York Press, 1991); Yohanan Friedmann, "Medieval Muslim Views of Indian Religions," *Journal of the American Oriental Society* 95 (1975), 214–21; Jacob Katz, *Exclusiveness and Tolerance*

(New York: Schocken Books, 1962); Steven S. Schwarzschild, "Do Noachites Have to Believe in Revelation?" *Jewish Quarterly Review* 52 (1962), 297–308; 53 (1963), 30–65; David Novak, *The Image of the Non-Jew in Judaism* (Toronto: Edwin Mellen Press, 1984); Arvind Sharma, "All Religions Are—Equal? One? True? Same?: A Critical Examination of Some Formulations of the Neo-Hindu Position," *Philosophy East and West* 29 (1979), 59–72; Arvind Sharma, ed., *Neo-Hindu Views of Christianity* (Leiden: E. J. Brill, 1988). An anthology that is invaluable for the study of other religious views of Christianity is Paul J. Griffiths, ed., *Christianity through Non-Christian Eyes* (Maryknoll: Orbis Books, 1990).

A standard and still reliable historical account of Christian doctrines about other religions is Louis Capéran, *Le Problème du salut des infidèles: Essai historique* (Toulouse: Grand Séminaire, 1934). Gerald H. Anderson stated recently that "there is no book in any language that provides a comprehensive study of Christian attitudes and approaches to people of other faiths throughout the history of Christianity" ("Christian Mission and Religious Pluralism: A Selected Bibliography of 175 Books in English, 1970–1990," *International Bulletin of Missionary Research* 14 [1990], 172). In response to this need, a multi-volume historical work, tentatively entitled *Christianity in Its Religious Contexts,* is in preparation under the general editorship of Frederick W. Norris working with a team of editors including Kees Bolle, Saphir Athyal, J. A. DiNoia, David Bundy, and Dana Robert. The standard historical account of the Christian missions is the work of Kenneth Scott Latourette, *A History of the Expansion of Christianity,* 7 vols. (New York: Harper & Row, 1945, Paternoster Press, 1971). More accessible is the one-volume work by Stephen Neill, *A History of Christian Missions,* revised for the second edition by Owen Chadwick (London: Penguin Books, 1986).

Many books in theology of religions begin with accounts of the history of such doctrines, but, as might be expected, these accounts reflect current lines of debate and are in varying degrees shaped to the constructive purposes of their authors. A broader perspective can be gained from discussions dispersed throughout the volumes of Jaroslav Pelikan's history of Christian doctrine at those points where he has endeavored to discuss the development of what are here described as doctrines about other religions. For these discussions, consult *The Christian Tradition* (Chicago: University of Chicago Press, 1971–89), vol. 1, 12–67; vol. 2, 199–215, 227–42; vol. 3, 34–42, 242–55; vol. 4, 240–44; 312–13; vol. 5, 101–17, 332–36.

Pelikan's account of the emergence of such doctrines in the period when the early Christian community sought to define itself first over against Judaism and then against the religiously teeming world of late antiquity has directly influenced the discussion of these issues in this book. For the judgment that the modern day Christian encounter with other religious communities is analogous to the situation of the early Christian community, see George A. Lindbeck, "The Sectarian Future of the Church," *The God Experience,* ed. Joseph P. Whelan (New York: Newman Press, 1971), 226–43. Studies that can be read as confirming this judgment are: Robin Lane Fox, *Pagans and Christians* (New York: Alfred A. Knopf, 1987); W. H. C. Frend, *The Rise of Christianity* (Philadelphia: Fortress Press, 1984); Wayne A. Meeks, *The Moral World of the First Christians* (Philadelphia: Westminster Press, 1986); Robert L. Wilken, *The Christians as the Romans Saw Them* (New Haven: Yale University Press, 1984). For a sociological description of the current situation, see Joseph H. Fichter, "Christianity as a World Minority," in *Christianity and the Wider Ecumenism,* ed. Peter C. Phan (New York: Paragon House, 1990), 59–72.

For the works of Justin and Clement referred to in this chapter, see *The Ante-Nicene Fathers,* ed. Alexander Roberts, James Donaldson, and Rev. A. Cleveland Coxe, 9 vols. (1884–86; rpt. Grand Rapids: Eerdmans, 1971), 1, 162–93; 2, 171–567. For Augustine, see *Concerning the City of God Against the Pagans,* trans. Henry Bettenson and ed. David Knowles (Baltimore: Penguin Books, 1972).

As a general comment on the entire history of the relations of Christianity to other religions, the following remark of John Milbank is especially illuminating: "[E]very major religion is *already* the result of a confronting of the fact of religious differences and an attempt to subsume such differences (although the ways and degrees of constructing 'universality' themselves vary enormously . . .). By comparison, genuinely local religions . . . may scarcely have had to confront the question of whether their beliefs and practices are relevant beyond the confines of their own society; this is presumably why they are so liable to conversion by or accommodation within the terms of a major religion, which is in part the result of such a confrontation. The major religions are notoriously not so susceptible to conversion or accommodation, precisely because they embody a more abstract, universal and deterritorialized cultural framework, although they do not usually succumb to the temptation of trying to found this universality in reason independent of all particularized memory" ("The End of Dialogue," in *Christian Uniqueness Reconsidered,* ed. Gavin D'Costa [Maryknoll: Orbis, 1991], 180).

Milbank's remark suggests, among other things, that it would be a mistake to exaggerate the novelty of the current situation of religious interaction. For a survey of the dawning of interest in other religions in the Enlightenment period, and a review of earlier discussion among Western philosophers and theologians, see Peter Harrison, *"Religion" and the Religions in the English Enlightenment* (Cambridge: Cambridge University Press, 1990). See also Frank E. Manuel, *The Eighteenth Century Confronts the Gods* (Cambridge: Harvard University Press, 1959). In his *Attitudes to Other Religions: Comparative Religion in Seventeenth- and Eighteenth-Century Britain* (Manchester: Manchester University Press, 1984), David Pailin remarks that "in most cases references to other religions in the theological writings of the 17th and 18th centuries are to be interpreted primarily with reference to contemporary discussions about the nature and verification of Christian belief" (6). For interest in and attitudes towards particular religious traditions, see: Albert Hourani, *Islam in European Thought* (Cambridge: Cambridge University Press, 1991); B. Z. Keder, *European Approaches towards the Muslims* (Princeton: Princeton University Press, 1988); Edward W. Said, *Orientalism* (New York: Panteon, 1978); Peter J. Marshall, ed., *The British Discovery of Hinduism in the Eighteenth Century* (Cambridge: Cambridge University Press, 1970); Henri de Lubac, *La recontre du Bouddhisme et de l'occident* (Paris: Aubier, 1952); and Philip C. Almond, *The British Discovery of Buddhism* (Cambridge: Cambridge University Press, 1988). For the view of Islam as a Christian heresy, see Norman Daniel, *Islam and the West* (Edinburgh University Press, 1958), 184–94, 246–48.

In the Catholic community, current theological debate about Christian doctrines about other religions received much of its impetus from the Second Vatican Council. A sense of the shape of the discussion in the immediate postconciliar period can be derived from Peter Schreiner, "Roman Catholic Theology and Non-Christian Religion," *Journal of Ecumenical Studies* 6 (1969), 376–99; James Dupuis, "The Salvific Value of Non-Christian Religions," in *Evangelization, Dialogue and Development*, ed. Mariasusai Dhavamony (Rome: Gregorian University Press, 1972); and George A. Lindbeck, *The Future of Roman Catholic Theology* (Philadelphia: Fortress Press, 1969). For recent commentary on the impact of the council's teaching on theology of religions, see René Latourelle, ed., *Vatican II: Assessment and Perspectives* (New York: Paulist Press, 1988–1990), vol. 3, 160–336.

In the 1988 reorganization of the central administration of the Catholic Church, the Secretariat for Non-Christians became the Pontifical

Council for Interreligious Dialogue (PCID) and was given a more permanent status within the Vatican. Since its establishment in 1964, this body has actively promoted dialogue at the local and international levels and collaborated with the World Council of Churches sub-unit on dialogue. The PCID *Bulletin* is an important source for papal statements on dialogue, for other documentation, and for theological essays. For an overall view of the significance of the PCID, see the collection of essays by its current prefect, African Cardinal Francis Arinze, *Church in Dialogue: Walking with Other Believers* (San Francisco: Ignatius Press, 1990). See also the essays by Marcello Zago, "Les Documents du Conseil Pontifical pour le dialogue interreligieux," *Bulletin* 72, XXIV (1989), 362–76, and "The Life and Activity of the Pontifical Council for Interreligious Dialogue," *Bulletin* 74, XXV (1990), 150–54. For a general statement of church policy and attitudes, see the PCID document, "The Attitude of the Church towards the Followers of Other Religions: Reflections and Orientations on Dialogue and Mission," *Bulletin* 56, XIX (1984), 126–41.

For a survey of WCC activities prior to Uppsala (1968), see Carl F. Hallencreutz, *New Approaches to Men of Other Faiths* (Geneva: World Council of Churches, 1970). For commentary on more recent developments, see John B. Carman, "Continuing Tasks in Interreligious Dialogue," *Ecumenical Review* 22 (1970), 199–209; Eugene Carson Blake, "Identity, Power and Community: Report of the General Secretary," *Ecumenical Review* 23 (1971), 105–17; Stanley J. Samartha, "Dialogue as a Continuing Christian Concern," *Ecumenical Review* 23 (1971), 129–42.

The interaction of religious communities is, of course, a far more complex affair than the setting of interreligious dialogue can reflect. For the purposes of the overall argument of this book, the dialogue setting throws into perspective the doctrinal issues that religious interaction generates when religious communities announce a public commitment to dialogue. The description of the logical features of interreligious dialogue is adapted from William A. Christian, Sr., *Oppositions of Religious Doctrines* (New York: Seabury, 1972), 17–27. Ninian Smart's *World Religions: A Dialogue* (Baltimore: Penguin Books, 1966) nicely exhibits the potential for doctrinal arguments afforded by this kind of interreligious conversation. Given the various meanings associated with the term "dialogue," it has been important to stipulate the sense in which the term is used in this book. As Eric J. Sharpe has noted: "One is sometimes almost forced to reflect that the cause of sympathetic inter-religious dialogue might be better served if the word were to be laid aside for a time. . . . [W]hen a single word can be used in such diverse senses, and serve the interests of attitudes involving distinctly different presuppositions (rational and non-rational), clearly some semantic tidying up is necessary" ("The Goals of Inter-Religious Dialogue," in *Truth and Dialogue,* ed. John Hick [London: Sheldon Press, 1974], 91).

The remote origins of the religious use of the notion of dialogue lay in the work of existentialist and personalist thinkers in the first quarter of the twentieth century. But, according to Sharpe, it was only after World War II that the notion came to be applied to interreligious relations ("Dialogue of Religions," in *Encyclopedia of Religion,* ed. Mircea Eliade [New York: Macmillan, 1987], vol. 4, 346; see also his *Comparative Religion: A History* [New York: Charles Scribner's Sons, 1975], 251–66). To be sure, interreligious conversations have had a long history. But, for a variety of reasons, in the mid-twentieth century interreligious relations came increasingly to be viewed in terms of interreligious dialogue. At the outset, the term "dialogue" and the stance it represented were championed principally by liberal Christians. Conservatives, according to Sharpe, "found the term unacceptable, since it implicitly placed religious traditions on a par with one another, or at least was less than explicit when it came to affirming the claims of Christianity" ("Dialogue of Religions," 346). While the notion of interreligious dialogue has steadily gained in legitimacy within mainstream Christianity since the mid-twentieth century, this apparent incompatibility between mission and dialogue has remained a source of tension in most Christian communities. The Second Vatican Council in effect simply juxtaposed the commitments to dialogue and mission without undertaking to show how, doctrinally speaking, they could be reconciled with each other.

Within this perspective, the significance of the two recent Vatican documents stands out sharply. First, in the encyclical *Redemptoris Missio,* Pope John Paul II reaffirms the church's commitment to dialogue and lists dialogue along with proclamation and witness as one of the "paths of mission" (see paragraphs 55–57; see also Cardinal Arinze's brief commentary on these paragraphs in his essay, "The Place of Dialogue in the Church's Mission: Reflection on *Redemptoris Missio,*" PCID *Bulletin* 76, XXVI [1991], 20–23). A second document, issued jointly by the PCID and the congregation for the Evangelization of Peoples, describes the church's commitment to dialogue as "firm and irreversible" and states that dialogue is "an integral element of the church's evangelizing mission" ("Dialogue and Proclamation: Reflections and Orientations on Interreligious Dialogue and the Proclamation of the Gospel of Jesus Christ" [paragraph 38], *Origins* 21 [1991], 128). Both *Redemptoris*

Missio and "Dialogue and Proclamation" can thus be viewed as addressing the problematic that underlies debate throughout the last quarter of this century concerning the compatibility of the embrace of dialogue with the missionary mandate. One of the objectives of this book has been to turn the church's attention to a newly emerging problematic: What is the impact (doctrinally and theologically) of the embrace of interreligious dialogue on traditional Christian theology of religions?

CHAPTER TWO: VARIETIES OF RELIGIOUS AIMS

Although the Second Vatican Council was itself a watershed in the history of the Catholic Christian community's relations with other religious communities, theological debate in this area had something of a slow start, perhaps because other issues seemed more pressing in the immediate wake of the council. As we have noted above, debate within Protestant Christian communities had been underway since the forties, largely in response to initiatives at the international level in such bodies as the World Council of Churches. During this period, the positions of two theologians on this topic came to occupy center stage, Karl Rahner on the Catholic side and Hendrik Kraemer on the Protestant side. The entire January 1989 issue of *The Ecumenical Review*, entitled "The Church and the World of Religions and Cultures: Kraemer in Retrospect," (41 [1989], 1 ff.) is devoted to assessing the impact of Kraemer's thought in Protestant circles. The debate on the Catholic side largely centered on Rahner's controversial notion of "anonymous Christianity." Out of the extensive literature on this topic, see Gavin D'Costa, "Karl Rahner's Anonymous Christians—A Reappraisal," *Modern Theology* 1 (1985), 131–48.

During the past decade, the field of Christian theology of religions has attracted the interest of many able philosophers and theologians, and witnessed the emergence of well-articulated proposals along relatively clearly defined lines. Since 1980, more than fifty books have appeared in English alone, and that figure does not include the hundreds of monographs that consider Christian relations with individual religious traditions. Recent works containing fairly complete bibliographies are Michael Barnes, *Christian Identity and Religious Pluralism* (Nashville: Abingdon Press, 1989); Gavin D'Costa, *Theology and Religious Pluralism* (Oxford: Basil Blackwell, 1986); and Glyn Richards, *Towards a Theology of Religions* (London: Routledge, 1989). For discussion of some recent books, see the review essays by Francis X. Clooney and Paul Knitter in *Religious Studies Review* 15 (1989), 197–207.

Gavin D'Costa has argued convincingly that the formula *extra ecclesiam nulla salus* has a properly intra-Christian use (see his "*Extra Ecclesiam Nulla Salus*—Revisited," in *Pluralism and Unbelief: Studies Critical and Comparative,* ed. Ian Hamnett [London: Routledge, 1990]). In his *Jesus Christ at the Encounter of World Religions* (Maryknoll: Orbis, 1991), Jacques Dupuis confirms this judgment: The formula "is borrowed from Fulgentius of Ruspe, who applies it not only to pagans but to Jews, and even to Christians who have separated themselves from the church, whether by schism or heresy. To culpably separate oneself from the church is tantamount to separating oneself from Christ. When the adage is cited in official texts of the magisterium as in the thirteenth century by the Creed of the Fourth Council of the Lateran (1215) and in the fourteenth century by the Bull *Unam Sanctam* (1302) of Boniface VIII, it seems to be intended to refer to those who find themselves outside the church voluntarily and culpably. The first text of the church magisterium explicitly to extend its usage beyond heretics and schismatics, to pagans and Jews, is the Decree for the Jacobites (1442) of the Council of Florence. In historical context, however, the primary intention of the council continues to be to apply the adage to those who have separated themselves from the church voluntarily and who have not reunited themselves to it before the end of their lives" (97).

Generally speaking, the concerns manifest in the current literature are similar to those of the immediate postconciliar period in that the central issue remains to account for the availability of salvation beyond the confines of the Christian community. Positions in the field are classified as exclusivist, inclusivist, and pluralist largely on the basis of their approaches to this issue. Thus, this typology figures prominently in such surveys as Alan Race, *Christians and Religious Pluralism* (Maryknoll: Orbis, 1982); Gavin D'Costa, *Theology and Religious Pluralism,* and "Theology of Religions," in *The Modern Theologians,* ed. David F. Ford (Oxford: Basil Blackwell, 1989), vol. 2, 274–90. A noteworthy difference between the current discussion and that immediately following the council is that pluralism seems to be displacing inclusivism as the prevailing approach within Christian theology of religions. The theology of Karl Rahner remains the most influential form of inclusivism, while John Hick has emerged as the chief exponent of pluralism.

It should be noted that, despite its widespread currency as a way of classifying the range of positions espoused in this area, the exclusivist/inclusivist/pluralist typology is by no means unchallenged. An important alternative classification employs the terms ecclesiocentrism, christocentrism, and theocentrism in combination with exclusivism and inclusivism (following the fourfold typology presented by J. Peter Schineller in "Christ and Church: A Spectrum of Views," *Theological Studies* 37 [1976], 545–66). For a representative discussion of this alternative typology, with references to the literature, see Jacques Dupuis, *Jesus Christ at the Encounter of World Religions,* 104–10. Although the alternative typology yields a somewhat more accurate classification of positions in the field of theology of religions, its complexity renders it unwieldy. More importantly—particularly when ecclesiocentrism is linked with exclusivism, christocentrism with inclusivism, and theocentrism with pluralism—the use of the labels ecclesiocentrism, christocentrism, and theocentrism implies that the doctrines of the Church, Christ, and God must compete for attention in theology of religions. Such typologizing obscures the more basic issue posed by current circumstances of religious interaction: how to affirm the universality of the Christian dispensation without sacrificing its particularity. As David Tracy recently remarked: "The new question is to find a way to formulate a Christian theological question on religious pluralism in such a manner that a genuinely new answer may be forthcoming without abandoning Christian identity. The 'answer' is unlikely to be, as some suggest, by shifting from a 'christocentric' to a 'theocentric' position. . . . For insofar as Christians know the God (as pure, unbounded Love) that all Christian models of theocentrism demand, they know *that* God in and through the decisive revelation of God in Jesus Christ" (*Dialogue with the Other* [Louvain: Peeters Press, and Grand Rapids: Eerdmans, 1990], 96–97). For analyses of the underlying issues, see the important essays by Rowan Williams ("Trinity and Pluralism"), Gavin D'Costa ("Christ, the Trinity and Religious Plurality"), and Christoph Schwöbel ("Particularity, Universality and the Religions") in *Christian Uniqueness Reconsidered,* ed. Gavin D'Costa, 3–46.

Even where the exclusivist/inclusivist/pluralist typology is not explicitly employed in interpreting the available options in the field, the soteriocentric principle prevails, though its empirical support seems to be eroding. Previously, theologians concerned to argue that all religious communities can be characterized as seeking salvation could appeal to such works as S. F. G. Brandon, *Man and His Destiny in the Great Religions* (Toronto: University of Toronto Press, 1962) and *The Savior God: Comparative Studies in the Concept of Salvation Presented to E. O. James* (Manchester: Manchester University Press, 1963); R. J. Z. Werblowsky and C. J. Bleeker, eds., *Types of Redemption* (Leiden: E. J. Brill, 1970). But for more recent comparative work questioning the cross-religious applicability of the category of salvation, see Willard G. Oxtoby,

"Reflections on the Idea of Salvation," *Man and His Salvation: Studies in Memory of S. G. F. Brandon,* ed. E. J. Sharpe and J. R. Hinnells (Manchester: Manchester University Press, 1973), 17–37, and Douglas Davies, "The Notion of Salvation in the Comparative Study of Religions," *Religion* 8 (1978), 85–100. Awareness of the diversity of ideas of salvation, though not necessarily abandonment of the soteriocentric assumption, is manifest in the *Studia Missionalia* collections devoted to studies of salvation in different religious traditions (Rome: Gregorian University Press, 1980 and 1981). John Hick continues to insist on the "sotertiological character of post-axial religion" in *An Interpretation of Religion: Human Responses to the Transcendent* (New Haven: Yale University Press, 1989), 21–69, in his interpretation of the empirical evidence.

The writings of Hendrik Kraemer—notably his *The Christian Message in a Non-Christian World* (London: Edinburgh House Press, 1938) and *Why Christianity of All the Religions* (London: Lutterworth Press, 1962)—are commonly taken to exemplify the exclusivist approach. The most sympathetic (though critical) discussion of Kraemer is D'Costa's in *Theology and Religious Pluralism,* 52–79, though it is confusing to find prospective accounts like that of George Lindbeck characterized by D'Costa as exclusivist here (79, note 64) and in "Theology of Religions" (276–78). This is a sign of the ambiguity of the typology (and of the unsatisfactoriness of framing the issues in these terms). Prospective accounts (like Lindbeck's and that advanced in this book) are proposed precisely to do justice to the full range of empirical, philosophical, and doctrinal factors, which standard exclusivist accounts deal with even less well than inclusivist and pluralist ones do. Exclusivism in the strict sense as defined in this book seems to be ruled out by the historic mainstream. A sign of this is that official teaching authorities in the Catholic Church ruled against application of the formula *extra ecclesiam nulla salus* to the state of non-Christians in their disposition of the Leonard Feeney case in 1949. Through an official letter to the archbishop of Boston (dated August 8, 1949), the Holy Office rejected Feeney's interpretation of the formula according to which salvation requires either de facto membership in the church or the explicit intention of joining it. For documentation, see Denzinger-Schönmetzer, 3866–73, and *The Christian Faith,* ed. J. Neuner and J. Dupuis (Staten Island: Alba House, 1981), nos. 854–57, and, for complete Latin and English texts of the letter, see *American Ecclesiastical Review* 127 (1952), 307–15.

Some form of inclusivism continues to be espoused by a wide range of authors. For examples, see discussions in Race, *Christians and Religious Pluralism,* 38–69, and Paul F. Knitter, who describes inclusivism as the

"Catholic model" in *No Other Name?* (Maryknoll: Orbis, 1985), 120–44. The inclusivist approach is best represented by Karl Rahner's influential essays on theology of religions in *Theological Investigations* (London: Darton, Longman & Todd, 1961-), notably: "Christianity and World Religions," vol. 5, 115–34; "Anonymous Christians," vol. 6, 390–98; "Observations on the Problem of the 'Anonymous Christian'," vol. 14, 280–94; "Jesus Christ in the Non-Christian Religions," vol. 17, 38–50. A fairly complete bibliography of Rahner's writings on this and related topics, and references to the extensive secondary literature can be found in C. J. Pedley, "An English Bibliographical Aid to Karl Rahner," *Heythrop Journal* 24 (1984), 319–65. For an influential critique of Rahner's position, see Hans Urs von Balthasar, *The Moment of Christian Witness* (Glen Rock, N.J.: Newman Press, 1968). For a spirited defense and critical reconstruction of a broadly Rahnerian inclusivism, see Gavin D'Costa, *Theology and Religious Pluralism,* 81–139. In his fine book, *Jesus Christ at the Encounter of World Religions,* Jacques Dupuis espouses a robust inclusivism, displaying all of the characteristic features of this type of theology of religions, including the endeavor to allow for the salvific value of other religions (see chapter 6 for a thorough survey of this discussion, and pages 147–51 for Dupuis's own position). D'Costa and Dupuis advance formidable arguments for inclusivism. If the terms in which the issues are currently framed are accepted, then Dupuis is surely right when he states, in the course of his critique of pluralism, that "an inclusive, open christocentrism remains possible and indeed represents the only way available to a Christian theology of religions truly worthy of the name" (108). The object of this book has been to field an alternative formulation of the issues.

There is a large body of broadly inclusivist literature in which "Christ" is taken to symbolize the fundamental aspirations common to all major religious traditions. There is a version of this approach in the last-mentioned of Rahner's essays above. Perhaps the most famous instance of this approach is Raimundo Panikkar's *The Unknown Christ of Hinduism* (London: Darton, Longman & Todd, 1964, and Maryknoll: Orbis Books, 1981); note the descriptive title of his more recent essay, "The Jordan, the Tiber and the Ganges: Three Kairological Moments of Christic Self-Consciousness," included in a volume advocating pluralist theology of religions and entitled *The Myth of Christian Uniqueness,* ed. John Hick and Paul F. Knitter (Maryknoll: Orbis Books, 1987). Another version of this approach is advanced by the Islamicist Kenneth Cragg in *The Christ and the Faiths* (Philadelphia: Westminster, 1986). See also S. J. Samartha, *One Christ—Many Religions* (Maryknoll: Orbis, 1991).

Decisive in the formation of most pluralist positions in theology of religions have been the writings of philosopher John Hick, most recently his *An Interpretation of Religion*. An up-to-date bibliography of Hick's works can be found in Gavin D'Costa, *John Hick's Theology of Religions: A Critical Evaluation* (Lanham, Maryland: University Press of America, 1987), 215–31. See also the critical study of Hick's theory of salvation by Chester Gillis, *A Question of Final Belief* (New York: St. Martin's Press, 1989). Although Wilfred Cantwell Smith can be regarded as advancing a broadly pluralist position—notably in his *Towards a World Theology* (Philadelphia: Westminster Press, 1981)—his stress on the centrality of personal faith over the historical identities of religious communities gives his position something of the flavor of what might be called a Muslim theology of religions. This impression is confirmed by his choice of the category "idolatry" to criticize non-pluralist positions in his essay, "Idolatry in Comparative Perspective," in Hick and Knitter, eds., *The Myth of Christian Uniqueness*, 53–68. Be that as it may, recent books clearly espousing pluralist positions in Christian theology of religions are: Paul Knitter, *No Other Name?* (where pluralism is termed the "theocentric model"), and Eugene Hillman, *Many Paths* (Maryknoll: Orbis Books, 1989).

Out of the many books that could be mentioned, the following would be particularly helpful in fostering a recognition of the varieties of aims religions foster even when the word salvation is employed to describe them. Consult in regard to the Buddhist, Muslim, and Judaic communities respectively: Nathan Katz, *Buddhist Images of Human Perfection* (Delhi: Motilal Banarsidass, 1982); Muhammad Abul Quasem, *Salvation of the Soul and Islamic Devotions* (London: Kegan Paul International, 1983); Frederick E. Greenspahn, ed., *The Human Condition in the Jewish and Christian Traditions* (Hoboken: KTAV Publishing House, 1986).

This chapter has argued that one way of rethinking the issue of the availability of salvation to non-Christian persons is to study the specification of patterns of life by aims of life. This discussion combines claims in philosophical ethics drawn from Thomas Aquinas, *Summa theologiae* 1a2ae, 1–5, with William A. Christian's philosophical analysis of the logic of practical doctrines.

The reading of Aquinas on these issues has been influenced by many sources, chiefly: the notes and appendices in the Blackfriars Edition of the *Summa theologiae* (New York: McGraw-Hill, and London: Eyre & Spottiswoode, 1974) by Thomas Gilby (vols. 16–19) and Anthony Kenny (vol. 22); Anthony Kenny, *Action, Emotion and Will* (London:

Routledge & Kegan Paul, 1963); Peter T. Geach, *Mental Acts: Their Content and Their Objects* (London: Routledge & Kegan Paul, 1957); G. E. M. Anscombe, "Modern Moral Philosophy," *Collected Philosophical Papers* (Minneapolis: University of Minnesota Press, 1981), vol. 3, 26–42; Alan Donagan, *Human Ends and Human Actions* (Milwaukee: Marquette University Press, 1985); Ralph McInerny, *Ethica Thomistica* (Washington, D.C.: The Catholic University of America Press, 1982); John Finnis, "Practical Reasoning, Human Goods and the End of Man," *New Blackfriars* 66 (1985), 438–51; Ralph McInerny, *Aquinas on Human Action* (Washington, D.C.: The Catholic University of America Press, 1992); Romanus Cessario, *The Moral Virtues and Theological Ethics* (Notre Dame: University of Notre Dame Press, 1991); and Lee H. Yearly, *Mencius and Aquinas: Theories of Virtue and Conceptions of Courage* (Albany: State University Press of New York, 1990).

The discussion of practical doctrines presupposes William A. Christian, *Meaning and Truth in Religion*, 60–77; *Oppositions of Religious Doctrines*, 43–59; *Doctrines of Religious Communities*, 5–11, 176–92; that on the relation of intentions to patterns of action owes much to Thomas Tracy, *God, Action and Embodiment* (Grand Rapids: Eerdmans, 1984), chapters 1 and 5. Emphasis on the varieties of aims of life commended by religious communities does not exclude the possibility that certain basic structures and outcomes of moral reasoning are common to all human beings and are manifest in the doctrines of their traditions. For discussion of this issue, see especially Ronald M. Green, *Religious Reason* (New York: Oxford University Press, 1978) and *Religion and Moral Reason* (New York: Oxford University Press, 1988), and John Finnis, *Natural Law and Natural Rights* (New York: Oxford University Press, 1980). The argument of this chapter suggests that even universally shared moral prescriptions are structured into distinctive patterns of life under the influence of religious (and transmoral) conceptions of the aim of life. In an important recent book in comparative religious ethics, John P. Reeder supports the view adopted here in showing how ethics and soteriology are intertwined in religious traditions, specifically, Judaism and Christianity, but potentially other traditions as well: *Source, Sanction and Salvation* (Englewood Cliffs: Prentice Hall, 1988). Reeder's concept of salvation is in many ways congruent with the concept of aim of life in this book. Reeder's notes provide a wide-ranging discussion of current positions in comparative religious ethics.

The illustration in this chapter is drawn from Theravadin Buddhist doctrines. It is offered as hypothetical for the reasons stated in chapter 5.

The illustration implies that the realization of the state of enlightenment involves recognition of the impermanence of the self and with it, presumably, the impossibility of interpersonal relations in the "post-earthly" state. The extent to which the doctrines of Buddhism (especially that of the "no-self") imply this extinction is a matter of considerable dispute. See, for example, Donald Swearer, "Bhikkhu Buddhadasa on Ethics and Society," *Journal of Religious Ethics* 7 (1979), 54–64, and G. L. Doore, "Religion within the Limits of the Quest for the Highest Good," *Religious Studies* 19 (1983), 345–59. See also Steven Collins, *Selfless Persons: Imagery and Thought in Theravada Buddhism* (Cambridge: Cambridge University Press, 1982). For an analysis of the question of how true oppositions among doctrines can arise and be recognized, see William A. Christian, *Oppositions of Religious Doctrines*, and, for the particular issue addressed in this chapter, *Doctrines of Religious Communities*, 125–44.

CHAPTER THREE: THE PROVIDENTIAL DIVERSITY OF RELIGIONS

It is as true now as it was in the past that the Christian community's relations with the Jewish community helped to set the direction for its relations with other religious communities. Thus the Second Vatican Council's Declaration on the Relationship of the Church to Non-Christian Religions was—in the initial stages of its conception—envisaged as a statement about Christian relations with the Jewish community. For a detailed history of the origins of this declaration and its extension to embrace the issue of the Church's relationship to other religions in addition to Judaism, see John M. Oesterreicher's introduction and commentary in *Commentary on the Documents of Vatican II*, ed. Herbert Vorgrimler (New York: Herder and Herder, 1969), vol. 3, 1–136. From the extensive literature on contemporary Jewish-Christian relations, see the helpful survey of some significant issues in Henry Siegmann, "A Decade of Catholic-Jewish Relations: A Reassessment," *Journal of Ecumenical Studies* 15 (1978), 243–60, and the response by Edward H. Flannery in the same issue, 503–11. See also Dupuis, *Jesus Christ at the Encounter of World Religions*, 118–24, with references to the extensive literature. One of the best books on this issue is David Novak, *Jewish-Christian Dialogue* (New York: Oxford University Press, 1989).

A recent letter of the Vatican Congregation for the Doctrine of the Faith discusses the extent to which Christians may learn from and adopt methods of prayer drawn from other religious traditions. For the text, see "Some Aspects of Christian Meditation," *Origins* 19 (1989), 492–98.

The conception of the logic of the doctrine of revelation advanced in this chapter is dependent on many sources, particularly the Second Vatican Council's "Constitution on Divine Revelation," *The Documents of Vatican II,* ed. Walter M. Abbott, 110–28. For the crucial distinction between the causal presence and the personal presence of God, see Aquinas, *Summa theologiae,* 1a. 8 and 43. It would be possible to read a major strand in the argument of Karl Barth's *Church Dogmatics,* ed. G. W. Bromiley and T. F. Torrance (Edinburgh: T. & T. Clark, 1936–69), as a commentary on the importance of this distinction, both in his early explicit discussion of the doctrine of revelation and, in subsequent volumes, his massive redescription of the Christian narrative. Barth can be read here, not as underplaying the role of the human in the Christian faith (as he is often construed), but as securing the specificity of the self-identifying ("special") revelation of God (in Aquinas's terms, his personal presence) from absorption as a permanent feature of human religious consciousness (in Aquinas's terms, the knowledge of God arising from his causal presence)—the fundamental weakness Barth perceived in many forms of nineteenth-century Protestant theology and in whose light he criticized Roman Catholic "natural theology." This reading of Barth is dependent upon Hans W. Frei, "The Doctrine of Revelation in the Thought of Karl Barth, 1909–1922: The Nature of Barth's Break with Liberalism," Ph.D. dissertation, Yale University (Ann Arbor: University Microfilms, 1956), and "An Afterword: Eberhard Busch's Biography of Karl Barth," in *Karl Barth in Re-View: Posthumous Works Reviewed and Assessed,* ed. H. Martin Rumscheidt (Pittsburgh: Pickwick Press, 1981), 95–116.

For revelation as the source of knowledge about the true aim of life, see *Summa theologiae,* 1a. 1 and 12; 2a2ae. 2, 2. Barth makes a similar point when he writes that we understand the "mountain" of knowledge in the light of vision; see his *Fides Quaerens Intellectum: Anselm's Proof for the Existence of God in the Context of his Theological Scheme* (Richmond: John Knox Press, 1960), 21. For the reading of the First Letter of John suggested, see Raymond E. Brown, *The Epistles of John* (Garden City: Doubleday, 1982), 381–97, 422–27. The notion of the "promise" of revelation is drawn from Ronald F. Thiemann, *Revelation and Theology: The Gospel as Narrated Promise* (Notre Dame: Notre Dame University Press, 1985). The view of revelation advanced here is compatible with the emphasis of recent theology on the fundamentally interpersonal and self-communicative structure of revelation. For discussion, see René Latourelle, *The Theology of Revelation* (Staten Island: Alba House, 1966), and Avery Dulles, *Models of Revelation* (Garden City: Doubleday, 1983). Divine *self-* communication does not exclude the communication of some knowledge about God and his purposes. See Paul Helm, *The Divine Revelation* (London: Marshall, Morgan & Scott, 1982), especially chapter 2; William J. Abraham, *Divine Revelation and the Limits of Historical Criticism* (New York: Oxford University Press, 1982), especially chapter 1; and David Brown, *The Divine Trinity* (LaSalle, Illinois: Open Court, 1985), chapter 2. On the notion of *sacra doctrina* and its bearing on the doctrine of revelation in Aquinas, see: Per Erik Persson, *Sacra Doctrina: Reason and Revelation in Aquinas,* trans. Ross Mackenzie (Philadelphia: Fortress Press, 1970); Gerald F. Van Ackeren, *Sacra Doctrina* (Rome: Catholic Book Agency, 1952); J. A. Weisheipl, "The Meaning of *Sacra Doctrina* in *Summa theologiae* I, q. 1," *Thomist* 38 (1974), 49–80; Thomas C. O'Brien, " 'Sacra Doctrina' Revisited: the Context of Medieval Education," *Thomist* 41 (1977), 475–509.

For the role of the initial religious conception of a community, see the discussions of basic religious suggestions in William A. Christian, Sr., *Meaning and Truth in Religion,* 93–112, 128, 193, 206–7, 238–41, 246–47, and "Some Uses of Reason," in *The Relevance of Whitehead,* ed. Ivor Leclerc (London: George Allen and Unwin, 1961), 53–55. On the particularistic universality of claims to truth (though without the use of this expression), see the discussion of the basic assumption of doctrinal schemes in J. M. Bochenski, *The Logic of Religion,* 58–62, and William A. Christian, Sr., "Bochenski on the Structure of Schemes of Doctrines," *Religious Studies* 13 (1977), esp. 216–19. For a discussion of many of the issues covered by the doctrine of revelation, see Christian's *Doctrines of Religious Communities,* chapter 4 and 5. For the idea that the doctrine of revelation can have a variety of "uses," see David H. Kelsey, *The Uses of Scripture in Recent Theology* (Philadelphia: Fortress Press, 1975).

The account of the doctrine of revelation advanced in this book represents an alternative to prominent inclusivist and pluralist uses of the doctrine in Christian theology of religions. For an account of the doctrine of revelation that has influenced inclusivist formulations of the role of general revelation, see especially Karl Rahner, *Foundations of Christian Faith* (New York: Seabury Press, 1978), 138–75. In this vein, see also Jacques Dupuis, *Jesus Christ at the Encounter of World Religions,* 152–77, which extends to include even a "theology of nonbiblical scriptures."

For a representative pluralist account of the doctrine of revelation, see Paul Knitter, *No Other Name?*, 209–10, and *passim* for his appraisal of exclusivist and inclusivist accounts.

Both inclusivist and pluralist accounts of general revelation endeavor, in varying degrees, to "de-particularize" the sources of religious truth. The motivation for this endeavor is trenchantly stated, for example, by Dupuis (99–104), who argues that, in order to overcome the "scandal of particularity" and to resolve the problems it poses, "an ecclesiological de-centering and a christological re-centering of theology of religions" (97) is needed. Dupuis is a representative inclusivist here in resisting the pluralist alternative in which both ecclesiocentrism *and* christocentrism must be made to yield to a theocentric perspective in accounting for the availability of religious truth and salvation to other religious communities. But Dupuis is prepared to qualify the ecclesiocentrism he discerns in standard forms of Catholic theology of religions and to move toward a more purely christocentric perspective. In contrast to Dupuis's proposal, the notion of particularistic universality advanced in this book binds christology and ecclesiology closely together. Christian theology of religions cannot adopt a perspective on the universal salvific will of God and the unique mediatorship of Jesus Christ that is independent of the promises that God entrusted first to Israel and then to the Church. In a way that is fundamentally mysterious, the salvation of the world depends on the fidelity of the Christian community to its living Lord. Only from within the context of the particularities of the incarnation, passion, death, resurrection, and glory of Jesus Christ *and* of the faithfulness and mission of the Church can Christian theology of religions speak with confidence about the availability of religious truth and the unlimited scope of salvation. Thus it is argued in this chapter that the notion of general revelation be conceived as an extension of special revelation, and not the other way around. See Aidan Nichols, *The Theology of Joseph Ratzinger* (Edinburgh: T & T Clark, 1988), 72–73, 153–54.

Also central to inclusivist and pluralist accounts of the sources of religious truth is a generalized concept of religious experience. There are good reasons to believe that a doctrinally specific account of religious experience is preferable to the more generalized one favored by inclusivist and pluralist positions. Such an account would attend to the specific experiences afforded by membership in a religious community and by the cultivation of its pattern of life rather than to the transcendental experience underlying the particularities of religious expression. See Louis Dupré's discussion of the specificity of religious experience in *The Other Dimension* (Garden City: Doubleday, 1972), 11–61. For a recent philosophical analysis of the concept, see Wayne Proudfoot, *Religious Experience* (Berkeley: University of California Press, 1985).

The account of religious experience presupposed in this chapter is closer to a cultural-linguistic than to an experiential-expressive approach to the concept (to use George Lindbeck's terms [*The Nature of Doctrine,* especially 30–45]). But the argument here does not depend on pressing this point, nor on preferring a broadly cultural-linguistic approach to religious experience. One could allow for more generalized (less doctrinally specific) accounts of religious experience, provided they did not blur important cross-religious variations in the doctrines by which religious communities identify the sources of the truth and rightness of their beliefs and practices. An obstacle to the development of a truly generalized concept of religious experience, for use in general theories of religion, is that the concept inevitably implies the experience of "something" and thus fits best into theistic contexts. This feature of the concept is exemplified in Karl Rahner, "Experience of Transcendence from the Standpoint of Christian Dogmatics," in *Theological Investigations,* vol. 18, 173–88. See also Nicholas Lash, *Easter in Ordinary: Reflections on Human Experience and the Knowledge of God* (Charlottesville: University Press of Virginia, 1988). A generalized concept of religious experience is central to John Hick's position; see *An Interpretation of Religion,* 129–71, for his effort to expunge the theistic connotations of the concept.

These problems come to the surface in discussions of the particular type of religious experience represented by mystical experience. Although accounts of mystical experience drawn from across the major religious traditions display certain common features, there is wide agreement among students of mysticism that the experiences of Hindu, Buddhist, Jewish, Muslim, and Christian mystics are shaped by specific traditions. For a general orientation to this perspective and its importance for understanding mysticism, see Louis Dupré, "Mysticism," in the *Encyclopedia of Religion,* ed. Mircea Eliade (New York: Macmillan, 1987), vol. 10, 245–61. For the religious specificity of mystical experiences, see the two volumes of essays edited by Steven Katz: *Mysticism and Philosophical Analysis* (New York: Oxford University Press, 1978) and *Mysticism and Religious Traditions* (New York: Oxford University Press, 1983). In a careful and philosophically rigorous study, Caroline Franks Davis has argued that, despite the scheme-specific character of mystical experiences, a broadly theistic (but doctrinally "relatively unramified") common core can be discerned in accounts of such experiences drawn from the major religious traditions, including nontheistic ones (*The Evidential Force of Religious Experience* [Oxford: Clarendon

Press, 1989], especially 166–92). As the title suggests, her work is a defense of the role of arguments from religious experience in mounting a cumulative case for theism. Within this framework, she must show that the conflicting descriptions of the object of religious experience embodied in scheme-specific accounts of religious mystics do not defeat an appeal to religious experience in arguments for theism. But given its high degree of doctrinal generality (190–91), this common core does not efface the significant doctrinal differences that obtain among the religious traditions whose adherents' mystical experiences Davis considers. This is important for the argument of this chapter. Even a relatively generalized account of religious/mystical experience (such as Davis's) avoids obscuring cross-religious variations in the highly ramified doctrines in which religious traditions identify the sources of the truth and rightness of their beliefs and practices.

The discussion of the doctrine of purgatory is dependent upon the following sources: Aquinas, *Summa Contra Gentes,* 4, 91–95 and *Summa theologiae,* Suppl. 69–70; Karl Rahner, "Purgatory," in *Theological Investigations,* vol. 19, 181–91; Joseph Ratzinger, *Eschatology: Death and Eternal Life,* trans. Michael Waldstein (Washington, D.C.: The Catholic University of America Press, 1988), 218–33. Reliable surveys of the doctrine are presented by A. Piolante, "Il Dogma del Purgatorio," *Euntes Docete* 6 (1953), 287–311, and, more accessibly, by R. J. Bastian, "Purgatory," *New Catholic Encyclopedia,* vol. 11, 1034–39. A study of the development of the doctrine from the patristic through the medieval periods is presented by Jacques LeGoff, *The Birth of Purgatory,* trans. Arthur Goldhammer (Chicago: University of Chicago Press, 1984). For a discussion of Rahner's position, see Peter C. Phan's *Eternity in Time: A Study of Karl Rahner's Eschatology* (Selinsgrove: Susquehanna University Press, 1988), 122–34. For discussion of the final significance of personal decisions in this life for the life to come, see Ratzinger, *Eschatology,* 205–9, and Germain Grisez, *The Way of the Lord Jesus: Christian Moral Principles* (Chicago: Franciscan Herald Press, 1983), 445–46. See Richard Swinburne's brief but intelligent discussion of purgatory in *Responsibility and Atonement* (Oxford: Clarendon Press, 1989) 197–98. On the limits of our knowledge of the life to come, see Karl Rahner, "The Hermeneutics of Eschatological Assertions," in *Theological Investigations,* vol. 4, 323–46.

The doctrine of purgatory, as applied to the postmortem state and destiny of the members of other religious communities, helps to overcome the speculative tone that inclusivist (e.g., D'Costa, *Theology and*

Religious Pluralism, 68) and pluralist (e.g., Knitter, *No Other Name?,* 117) critics sometimes find in prospective accounts of the salvation of non-Christians. Purgatory provides, for Christians and non-Christians alike, a "painful" interval in which an assured (even if not fully anticipated) enjoyment is deferred for lack of readiness or preparation. There are many instances of self-imposed deferments in ordinary life. The Christian doctrine of purgatory allows for the possibility of the divine provision of such a deferment for those who die justified (in the liturgy, they are described as "holy souls") but still in need of additional transformation or purification across the whole range of their affective and intellectual capacities. Reformation and Orthodox theologians who find the argument of this chapter appealing but who have confessional objections to the doctrine of purgatory could content themselves with a less specified notion of prospective salvation or with an alternative account of what it might entail.

In "Human Diversity and Salvation in Christ," *Religious Studies* 20 (1984), 590, Grace Jantzen objects to prospective or eschatological accounts of the salvation of non-Christians on the grounds that they posit an implausible—because utterly discontinuous—transformation of persons in the life to come. This is an important objection. But it does not seem fatal to the approach being suggested here: the doctrine of purgatory envisages the possibility that, even for Christians, the transition to bliss will be "revolutionary," so to speak, and not merely in a cognitive sense. The enjoyment of the vision of God is deferred precisely in order to permit further transformation of persons who, for whatever reasons, are not yet ready for it. There is nothing to say that the required transformation will not be of a radical kind. On the other hand, in response to Kenneth Surin's complaints about the "subsequence theory" that prospective accounts seem to involve (see " 'Many Religions and the One True Faith': on Lindbeck's Chapter Three," *Modern Theology* 4 [1988], 187–209), it can be said that the doctrine of purgatory does not envisage a sharp, temporal disjunction between earthly life and the life to come. On the contrary, the doctrine of purgatory supposes a real continuity: a link obtains between purgation in this life and purgation in the next, although (according to Aquinas) the former is willingly undertaken or embraced and the latter is more passively endured. The doctrine need not be understood to entail a strictly temporally extended period "between" life on earth and the life to come. The doctrine of purgatory simply allows for some kind of interval in which the necessary purification can be undergone by persons who die in the "state of grace," with their sins forgiven, but with lingering effects of sin or any other spiritual deficiencies (cognitive and affective) rendering them still unfit for the enjoyment of blissful, eternal fellowship with the Triune God.

CHAPTER FOUR: THEOLOGY IN DIALOGUE

In order to rise to the occasion afforded by interreligious dialogue, Christian theologians need to develop arguments for primary Christian doctrines that will articulate their claim to truth and rightness and respond to similar claims advanced by other religious communities. For a rigorously argued account of the importance of such conversations, see Paul J. Griffiths, *An Apology for Apologetics: On the Logic of Interreligious Dialogue* (Maryknoll: Orbis, 1991). See also William C. Placher, *Unapologetic Theology: A Christian Voice in a Pluralistic Conversation* (Louisville, Kentucky: Westminster/John Knox Press, 1989), 143–49. For a response to an earlier published version of the argument of this chapter, see Francis X. Clooney, "Vedanta, Theology and Modernity: Theology's New Conversations with the World's Religions," *Theological Studies* 51 (1990), 268–85.

Arguments in support of the Christian reference to the Triune God and of the predications about him expressed in primary doctrines have a central place in theology in dialogue. The employment of such arguments in the new interreligious conversation depends at least in part on understanding how they came to be eclipsed by the critique of skeptical western philosophers since the Enlightenment. Thus the argument of this chapter has been supplemented by an examination of certain broad trends in the history of philosophical theology.

In *Knowing the Unknowable God: Ibn-Sina, Maimonides, Aquinas* (Notre Dame: University of Notre Dame Press, 1986), David Burrell examines influential Muslim, Judaic, and Christian versions of referential arguments. For helpful discussions of Aquinas, see Brian Davies, *Thinking about God* (London: Geoffrey Chapman, 1985); P. T. Geach, "Aquinas," in *Three Philosophers,* ed. G. E. M. Anscombe and P. T. Geach (Ithaca: Cornell University Press, 1961), 69–125; Thomas C. O'Brien, *Metaphysics and the Existence of God* (Washington, D.C.: The Thomist Press, 1960). On the theological setting and force of arguments for the existence of God, see Karl Rahner, "Observations on the Doctrine of God in Catholic Dogmatics," in *Theological Investigations,* vol. 9, 127–44, and Walter Kasper, *The God of Jesus Christ* (New York: Crossroad, 1984), 65–79. For discussion of the range of tradition-specific names for God, see Peter C. Phan, "God as Holy Mystery and the Quest for God-equivalents in Interreligious Dialogue," *Irish Theological Quarterly* 55 (1989), 277–90.

In "The Migration of Theistic Arguments: From Natural Theology to Evidentialist Apologetics" (in *Rationality, Religious Belief and Moral Commitment,* ed. Robert Audi and William J. Enright, [Ithaca: Cornell University Press, 1986], 38–81), Nicholas Wolterstorff documents a thesis advanced in this chapter when he shows how referential arguments came loose from their theological moorings. For an extensive discussion of this topic, see Michael J. Buckley, *At the Origins of Modern Atheism* (New Haven: Yale University Press, 1987), and Nicholas Lash's discussion of the book in "When Did the Theologians Lose Interest in Theology?" in *Theology and Dialogue,* ed. Bruce Marshall (Notre Dame: University of Notre Dame Press, 1990), 131–47. Two books by James Collins also describe these developments: *God in Modern Philosophy* (Chicago: Regnery, 1959) and *The Emergence of the Philosophy of Religion* (New Haven: Yale University Press, 1967). For a discussion of the emergence of reductive accounts of religion, see J. Samuel Preus, *Explaining Religion* (New Haven: Yale University Press, 1987). My reading of the impact of the Kantian critique of metaphysics is dependent on Hans W. Frei, "Niebuhr's Theological Background," in *Faith and Ethics,* ed. Paul Ramsey (New York: Harper & Bros., 1957), 9–64, and Allen W. Wood, *Kant's Rational Theology* (Ithaca: Cornell University Press, 1978). See also Francis S. Fiorenza, *Foundational Theology* (New York: Crossroad, 1984), 250–84. For a telling critique of the subjective turn in theology, see Fergus Kerr, *Theology after Wittgenstein* (Oxford: Basil Blackwell, 1986). See also, Benedict Ashley, *Theologies of the Body* (Braintree, Massachusetts: The Pope John Center, 1985). For a philosophical perspective on the complexity of the turn to the subject, see Charles Taylor, *Sources of the Self: The Making of Modern Identity* (Cambridge: Harvard University Press, 1989), and James J. Buckley, "A Return to the Subject: The Theological Significance of Charles Taylor's Sources of the Self," *Thomist* 55 (1991), 497–509.

There has been considerable debate about the role of analogy in the thought of Aquinas. My reading of him has been influenced by many sources, chiefly: David Burrell, *Analogy and Philosophical Language* (New Haven: Yale University Press, 1973); William J. Hill, *Knowing the Unknown God* (New York: Philosophical Library, 1971); Ralph McInerny, *The Logic of Analogy* (The Hague: Martinus Nijhoff, 1971), and "Analogy and Foundationalism in Aquinas," in *Rationality, Belief and Religious Commitment,* ed. Audi and Wainwright, 271–88; Colman E. O'Neill, "Analogy, Dialectic and Interconfessional Theology," *Thomist*

47 (1983), 43–65; Gregory Rocca, "The Distinction Between *Res Significata* and *Modus Significandi* in Aquinas's Theological Epistemology," *Thomist* 55 (1991), 173–97. For a fuller discussion, see J. A. DiNoia, "Knowing and Naming the Triune God: The Grammar of Trinitarian Confession," in *Speaking the Christian God,* ed. Alvin F. Kimel (Grand Rapids: Eerdmans, 1992).

Pluralist accounts of references and predications turn out upon examination to be markedly nonpluralistic. See Placher, *Unapologetic Theology,* 143, and J. A. DiNoia, "Pluralist Theology of Religions: Pluralistic or Non-Pluralistic?" in *Christian Uniqueness Reconsidered,* ed. Gavin D'Costa, 119–34. See also D'Costa's discussion of John Hick in *Theology and Religious Pluralism,* 23–46. See also L. Philip Barnes, "Relativism, Ineffability and the Appeal to Experience: A Reply to the Myth Makers," *Modern Theology* 7 (1990), 101–14.

Index

Printed in the United States
129923LV00004B/9/A